Food Plants: Answers That Work

Food Plants: Answers That Work

Ken Reeves

Clarke, Irwin & Company Limited
Toronto/Vancouver

Illustrations by Deborah Drew-Brook

Canadian Cataloguing in Publication Data

Reeves, Ken, 1923-
  Food plants

Includes index.
ISBN 0-7720-1253-9

1. Vegetable gardening. 2. Fruit-culture.
I. Title.
SB318.R43   635   C80-094210-8

© 1980 Clarke, Irwin & Company Limited
ISBN: 0-7720-1253-9

1 2 3 4 5 6   85 84 83 82 81 80
Printed in Canada

This book is dedicated to my brother Frank; my sister Florence; and my cousin Kenneth C.; without whose help in time of crisis it would never have been written.

Acknowledgements

I gratefully acknowledge my son John, my daughter-in-law Fern, my son Robert and other members of our staff at Reeves Florist and Nursery in Woodbridge who effectively were "minding the store" while I became a recluse to write this book.

Contents

Introduction

The highlight of my summer holidays as a boy was preparing for the Canadian National Exhibition in Toronto. Not only did my father love growing vegetables, he also loved exhibiting them. He believed that exhibiting the very best vegetables in competitions benefitted the consumer and the grower alike. One reason he grew so many different kinds of vegetables was so that he would have a wide selection for the C.N.E. competition.

He came by this trait honestly. Both my paternal and maternal grandfathers were on the charter committee that began the Royal Agricultural Winter Fair in Toronto, which has become the showplace of the elite in agriculture in North America. However, the C.N.E. in late August offered the greater potential for exhibiting vegetables. Most vegetable crops in Southern Ontario were at their peak and timing was critical. For the two or three weeks prior to opening, the search for the best began. Those specimens with potential were carefully marked and woe betide the person who carelessly harvested them for market.

I can vividly remember a scrap between two schoolboy workers that resulted in one throwing a prize cauliflower at another. He missed his antagonist and this gorgeous white cauliflower was smashed against a door frame. Everyone was concerned that my father would react just as violently against the offender. Competition was keen and a second string cauliflower could cost the prize. We should have known him better, for violence was just not his way. There was a reprimand and that was it. It was the violent reaction of the young worker that is vivid in my memory because I saw so little of that kind of reaction at home.

Just as Dad loved to grow vegetables and fruit, Mother loved to prepare them. There were always at least two vegetables at every main meal and usually three. And while the rest of us ate the usual breakfast fare, Mother would have a cold asparagus and mayonnaise sandwich.

My inclinations were, however, more mechanical than horticultural. My first agricultural engineering marvel came about when I was fifteen. It was a monkey wrench marriage of an old 1929 Chev truck, a rear end out of a 1927 Studebaker and a couple of transmissions of uncertain pedigree. The result was to be a tractor to pull the potato digger. The first trial run, after weeks of greasy clothes and barked knuckles, was interesting. I had put the rear end in upside down. It would crawl forward at less than two miles per hour and reverse at close to seventy. My mechanical "talent" was eventually put to work building and equipping greenhouses.

One of my earliest experiments with growing was with compost and its effect on soil and growth. When you read later about turning compost, know that I have had many a free sauna on hot summer's day turning steaming compost by the truckload.

The response to a question of tieing cauliflower to keep them white also comes from thousands and thousands of repetitions of that operation. All I need to do now is assume the cauliflower-tieing stoop for a half an hour and my back seizes up from the damage done during those cold wet days of fall.

The questions that are answered in this book come from three sources: a weekly live phone-in over C.B.C. Radio Noon Toronto, which generates questions from southern and central Ontario plus New York and Pennsylvania. Our own retail nursery in Woodbridge, Ontario, is sought out by many looking for information on plant problems. My own garden produces questions as well as food for the table.

Many of the answers come from my personal experience growing plants, using knowledge passed down from three generations involved in commercial horticulture. Where I have not had this actual experience, I have gone to people who have. Growers have been most generous of their time and knowledge in their area of expertise.

The same has been true of the horticultural scientists and university extension people in both Canada and the United States. Their papers and verbal assistance have helped unravel many a plant problem. I hope I have done an effective job of communicating their knowledge to the home gardener.

Indeed, one of the unique features of this book is a complete list of government bulletins written by horticultural scientists on food plant subjects published in Canada and the north eastern United States. I believe this information deserves wider dissemination. The alphabetical listing by topics will provide you with a source of authoritative information that is specifically written for your local area. The list also opens the possibility of obtaining information that is not available locally.

My father would smile if he were living now and heard me as I reach back in memory and attempt to marry his growing techniques to the latest cultural methods as I answer these questions. The son, whose instinct was to reach for an adjustable wrench, has become everyman's gardener.

Chapter 1: Preparing Your Garden for Food Plants

Suitable Soil for Vegetables

I would like to plant a vegetable garden. How can I tell whether the soil I have is suitable for this?

If the area is presently in grass, this grass should be removed by lifting a thin layer of sod. Dig out a shovel depth of the soil under the sod to see what kind of soil you are dealing with.

I think my soil is hopeless. It's almost sand.

Sand can be converted into reasonable soil by adding a lot of peat moss — up to two parts peat moss to one part sand. However, you may find it less expensive to bring in 13 to 15 cm (5 to 6 in) depth of good topsoil and make your garden on top of the existing sand.

Rarely does a homeowner find rich soil under that green carpet of grass surrounding the home. Most urban areas were once established to supply the needs of a farm economy. As the community grew and extended its streets and services, it destroyed the soil that made its existence possible in the first place.

The first step is to sink a spade deep into the garden site and discover what lies beneath the surface. In the case of our questioner, sand lay beneath. Massive infusions of organic matter (peat moss, manure, compost) will give sand the capability of holding moisture and plant nutrients. Generally 13 to 15 cm (5 to 6 in) of good soil is required for a thriving garden and if your basic beginning is sand, then at least half of this depth should be peat moss and/or compost. Manure could be part of your sand-amending formula but because of its chemical content, it cannot be used as extensively without burning — 3 to 5 cm (1 to 2 in) is the most I would apply. The rest of the organic matter should be peat moss which contains no chemicals that can burn.

If the downward thrust of your spade meets stubborn resistance, then you have either clay subsoil or clay topsoil to challenge you. You need to know exactly what you are dealing with. If indeed it is subsoil, then you would be well advised to import some good garden loam (topsoil) for your vegetable garden. It will pay good dividends. If in doubt, take a sample to a reputable soil-testing lab or local nursery for evaluation (see pages 17 to 18).

It is the nature of clay topsoils to become hard when dry and sticky and impossible to work with when wet. If this is what you have, then you need the same massive applications of organic matter

11

outlined for sandy soils. With clay soils, the organic matter increases drainage, decreases the stickiness and makes the soil more workable in dry spells.

If you decide the soil you have can be amended to make a good garden plot, skim off the top 3 cm (1 in) of soil and put it in the compost. While thorough digging will break up the soil, you will be struggling with tufts of grass all summer unless you remove the very top layer.

Hand-digging or rototilling are both effective and should be done after the sod has been removed and before the organic matter or new topsoil is applied. If you have decided you must go the route of bringing in topsoil, simply dig the area, sod and all, and put the topsoil on top of the cultivated subsoil. This will raise the grade but there is no objection to this from a growing standpoint.

Soil Preparation

When is the best time to dig up the soil for a vegetable garden? In the fall when the crops are finished or in the spring?

I believe fall digging, rototilling or ploughing is best.

Do you have to remove all of the old tree leaves lying on top first?

A commercial farmer would run a disc over the crop residue in the summer, knocking it down and cutting it up. He would then apply manure, plough everything under and cultivate it thoroughly for the rest of the growing season to kill the weeds and grasses and to have the land ready for spring planting. However, with a small garden it is better to remove the crop residue, tree leaves, sod and other vegetation and compost it (see pages 26 to 30.)

What if I do have to wait until spring?

Then you will have to accelerate the process by starting early, as soon as the ground is frost-free and dry enough to work without being sticky. Don't be concerned about the root systems of the former vegetation. With adequate preparation and cultivation, these will soon break down and pose no real problem. The only exceptions would be the stiff, thick white roots of twitch grass and other perennial weeds like dandelions. These should be removed to the compost heap along with the sod from the surface. If they are not removed, you will be struggling with twitch grass and perennial weeds all summer.

Fall digging or rototilling is particularly beneficial with clay soils. There is no need to break down the clods of soil. Leave it open and lumpy. The frost will break down the most stubborn clods into a

12

friable, granular texture. Then all that is usually required in the spring is a light cultivation and the garden is ready.

A good garden soil that grows above-average crops is rich in bacteria, microbes and nitrogen needed to break down garden residues and tree leaves. It can digest great amounts of raw organic matter without composting them first. However, be warned that tomato plants and other vegetables are sometimes difficult to incorporate in the soil without big power equipment.

If your garden plot is new or old and infertile, you are best to remove all surface garden waste and compost it before returning it to the garden. Infertile soil is slow to break down raw garden wastes and these wastes can rob the plants of nutrients while they are in the process of decomposing.

Vegetation can also be killed chemically by one application of a herbicide containing the active ingredients of paraquat diquat. The material goes inert a few hours after the herbicide is applied to the soil so that there is no residual action to be concerned about. It effectively kills all green vegetation within twenty-four to forty-eight hours and the area is then ready to be cultivated. If there are tall weeds or grass, it would be a good idea to run a rotary lawn mower over them to reduce them to manageable size before using the herbicide.

Caution: Paraquat diquat is a toxic material. Care should be taken during application to avoid skin contact. Read all labels and wear rubber gloves. While the herbicide goes inert after it comes in contact with the soil, foliage sprayed with the chemical is poisonous to man and beast.

Light Requirements of Vegetable Gardens

I have just moved into a new house and would like to put in a vegetable garden. Can I put it anywhere it is convenient?

The prime requirement to grow vegetables successfully is direct sunlight for a minimum of half a day. All day is even better.

Succulent, flavourful vegetables gain their nutrition value from the energy they draw from direct sunlight. Without direct sunlight for at least half a day, a vegetable garden is a very doubtful enterprise. So before you lift a spade, observe the pattern of sunlight and shadow as the sun goes through its orbit and put your vegetable garden where it will get the maximum direct sunlight. Only those vegetables where the harvest is their leaves (lettuce, celery) can be grown with reasonable success in very bright indirect light.

High Density Vegetable Spacing

I would like to have a vegetable garden in my backyard but I don't have very much space. Is it still possible to get a decent crop?

One technique that will increase the productivity of the soil is double-depth digging. Under most cultivation techniques soil will eventually develop a hard pan layer at the deepest point of your digging, ploughing and particularly rototilling. One objective of double-depth cultivation is to break that hard pan and allow deeper root penetration.

If I do this will I get more plants in a smaller area?

Yes. The soil will then be able to support high density vegetable spacing. The plants touch in all directions at maturity and act as their own mulch. This cuts out light reaching the soil, eliminating much of the weeding necessary in wider row cropping. Moisture is also preserved.

When should I do this double digging?

I would do it in the fall. This is also the best time to do a soil test. Any fertilizer amendments can be done prior to spring cultivation.

1

2

Double-depth digging
1. Dig out a trench 30 cm (12 in) wide and to the depth of the topsoil or 30 cm (12 in), whichever comes first. Move this soil to the far end of the vegetable plot.
2. Dig and loosen the soil in the bottom of the trench as deep as possible. Leave the soil rough.

3

3. Dig a 30 cm (12 in) width next to this trench and turn this soil over into the original trench, mixing manure or compost as you go. Try to get the compost or manure vertically integrated into the mixture.

North American agriculture has generally substituted acreage for intensity. Land was plentiful and it was easier and cheaper to plant more acres to get more food. With the larger lots that homes used to be built on, the home gardener tended to do the same as the farmer. However, most homes now have smaller lots and less space for a vegetable and fruit garden. The answer is to intensify. This can be done by preparing the soil by double digging.

The technique involves some hard work but the results, particularly on heavier soils, are gratifying indeed. Begin by digging a trench the width of your plot, 30 cm (12 in) wide and to the depth of the topsoil or 30 cm deep (12 in), whichever comes first. This soil is removed to the far end of your plot. At this point you have a trench across one end of the plot and a mound of soil across the other end.

Now dig out the bottom of the trench, to a depth of 30 cm (12 in) if possible. In clay soil this may be difficult and should give you greater empathy for the plant root systems which try to penetrate this mass. Do not attempt to reduce this soil to a fine texture — 5 to 10 cm (2 to 4 in) clods are acceptable. If you can't reach the full depth due to the hardness of the subsoil, be satisfied with less.

The next step is to dig the next 30 cm (12 in) of topsoil and throw it over into the first trench, turning under any manure or compost. The objective is a quarter turn of the soil so that the compost or manure is more vertical than horizontal. Do not be concerned about reducing the clods to plantable size. The frost during winter will do this.

Repeat this process down the length of the plot and fill the mound of soil dug out of the first trench into the last. If you do not have available either manure or compost then add peat moss to obtain the necessary organic matter.

SPACING FOR HIGH DENSITY VEGETABLES

	Distance between plants in row		Distance between rows	
	cm	in	cm	in
*BEANS	5	2	46	18
*BEETS	2.5	1	30	12
CABBAGE (early)	46	18	46	18
CABBAGE (late)	61	24	61	24
*CARROTS	2.5	1	30	12
CAULIFLOWER (early)	46	18	46	18
CAULIFLOWER (late)	61	24	61	24
CELERY	15	6	30	12
CHARD, SWISS	30	12	46	18
CHINESE CABBAGE	30	12	46	18
CORN (early)	23	9	46	18
CORN (late)	30	12	61	24
CUCUMBERS	30	12	122	48
EGGPLANT	61	24	61	24
KOHLRABI	10	4	30	12
*LEEKS	15	6	46	18
LETTUCE (HEAD)	30	12	30	12
LETTUCE (LEAF)	30	12	30	12
MELON (HONEYDEW)	30	12	152	60
MUSKMELON (CANTALOUPE)	30	12	152	60
*ONIONS (GREEN, SEEDS OR SETS)	2.5	1	20	8
*ONIONS (COOKING, SEEDS OR TRANSPLANTS)	5	2	20	8
ONIONS (SPANISH)	15	6	25	10
PARSLEY	10	4	25	10
*PARSNIPS	2.5	1	46	18
*PEAS	2.5	1	46	18
PEPPERS	45	18	46	18
POTATOES	30	12	61	24
PUMPKINS	61	24	244	96
*RADISHES	2.5	1	15	6
RHUBARB	61	24	91	3
SPINACH	10	4	15	6
SQUASH	60	24	244	96
TOMATO (STAKED)	60	24	61	24
TOMATO (UNSTAKED)	99	39	99	39
TURNIPS (RUTABAGAS)	15	6	46	18
WATERMELONS	30	12	122	48

*In full sun all day and fertile soil, two and sometimes three plants can be successfully matured in this amount of space in a row.

Soil Analysis

I have heard that you can get soil samples analysed by soil-testing labs. Is this a good idea? Where should I send the sample?

Yes. A soil analysis is an excellent way to measure the various elements essential for good plant growth. Most provinces operate soil-testing labs at agricultural universities and colleges.

How much soil should I send?

You should send a composite sample of the soil — 227 mL (1/2 pt) is sufficient. Most soil-testing labs will also make a recommendation for granular fertilizer which should be applied at the time of soil preparation. This application generally lasts the life of the crop.

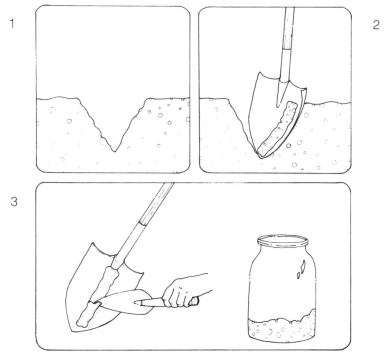

Soil sampling method
1. To take samples, use a clean shovel. Clear away surface litter and dig a V-shaped hole 15 cm (6 in) deep.
2. Take a 2.5 cm (1 in) slice down one side the full depth of the hole.
3. Trim the top and bottom of the slice to leave a 2.5 cm (1 in) width of soil. Place this entire sample in a clean container and add three to five samples taken in the same manner from different places in the garden. Mix thoroughly, removing any stones or debris. Send 227 mL (half a pint) to a soil-testing lab. If sampling a trouble spot, confine samples to the area giving the problem.

SOIL TEST LABS BY PROVINCE

ALBERTA   Fee: $2.00
   Agricultural Soil & Feed Testing Lab
   O.S. Longman Building
   6909-116 Street
   Edmonton, Alberta
   T6H 4P2

BRITISH COLUMBIA

   Regular Soil Test: $5.00
   Salts Conductivity and pH: $2.00

   Department of Agriculture
   Soil Testing Lab
   1873 Spall Road
   Kelowna, British Columbia
   V1Y 4R2

MANITOBA   Fee: $7.00

   (Ask for regular and sulphur tests)

   Provincial Soil Testing Laboratory
   University of Manitoba
   262 Ellis Building
   Winnipeg, Manitoba
   R3T 2N2

NEW BRUNSWICK
   Agricultural Laboratory
   New Brunswick Department of
      Agriculture
   P.O. Box 6000
   Fredericton, New Brunswick
   E3B 5H1

NEWFOUNDLAND
   Agriculture Canada
   Research Station Soil Analysis Lab
   P.O. Box 7098
   St. John's West, Newfoundland
   A1E 3Y3

NOVA SCOTIA
   Department of Agriculture
   Soil Testing Lab
   P.O. Box 550
   Truro, Nova Scotia
   B2N 5E3

ONTARIO
   Soil Test Laboratory
   Department of Land Resource
      Science
   University of Guelph
   Guelph, Ontario
   N1G 2W1

PRINCE EDWARD ISLAND
   Prince Edward Island Soil and Feed
      Testing Lab
   Research Station
   Box 1600
   Charlottetown, Prince Edward Island
   C1A 7N3

SASKATCHEWAN   Fee $9.00
   Department of Agriculture
   Soil Test Lab
   University of Saskatchewan
   Saskatoon, Saskatchewan
   S7N 0W0

QUEBEC   Fee $8.50
   Soil Test Laboratory
   Box 331
   McDonald College
   Ste Anne de Bellevue, Quebec
   H9X 1C0

Organic vs. Inorganic Fertilizers

I need to fertilize my vegetable garden but I would just as soon not use a lot of chemical fertilizers. Can I use organic material instead? Is it just as effective?

Plants require several major chemical elements to thrive. Three of these major elements — nitrogen, phosphorus and potash — must be added to the soil as fertilizers. Organic sources of these elements are bone and blood meal, manure, processed sewage sludge, fish fertilizer, seaweed, and composted garden and kitchen wastes. All the nutrients in these organic sources must be converted in the soil to chemical solutions which will then be picked up by the plant's root system.

So do they not work as quickly as chemical fertilizers?

The analysis generally is quite low and the nutrient content often very slowly soluble. Bone meal contains approximately 2 per cent nitrogen, 11 per cent phosphorus and no potash. The nitrogen and phosphorus must be decomposed by micro-organisms to soluble salts in the presence of oxygen and moisture before the plant's roots can absorb them. This process takes time, depending on the soil temperature, the amount of soil and number of micro-organisms present, and the oxygen and moisture content of the soil. If you applied bone meal this year, it may not be decomposed and available to the plant until the next growing season. On the positive side, however, this means it can be applied without fear of burning the roots. It is fertilizer soluble salts in excessive concentrations near the roots that cause burning.

What is the best kind of organic material to use for the fastest results?

I believe coarse, fibrous peat moss offers the greatest structural soil improvement potential for your dollars spent of any readily available organic material. It's almost impossible to overdo it, particularly in a new garden. Peat moss, however, does not contain plant nutrients.

A 170 dm³ (6 ft³) plastic bag of compressed peat moss will cover approximately 3 m² (10 ft²) of area 3 cm (1 in) deep. Check bargains in peat moss carefully. Peat moss packed by reputable suppliers is compressed two to one. One way of reducing the price is to reduce the compression, putting less in the bag. Feel the bag to check the firmness and make certain you get value for your money.

Once peat moss has been applied, repeat digging or rototilling at least once and preferably two or three times to thoroughly mix soil and organics. If you are just beginning soil improvement, don't get discouraged. Each year you will need to add lesser amounts of organic matter and the job will get easier.

Combined with the soil, organic ingredients open up the soil particles, allowing rapid root penetration. In addition this makes air spaces in the soil which supply the roots with essential oxygen. This, plus drainage potential and ease in cultivation, all help to ensure a successful vegetable garden.

Manure Can Burn Roots

I planted about seventy-five raspberry canes late this spring. Some of them have gone brown and are dying. Is this a virus disease?

Did they start to leaf out and then die back?

Yes, they came on beautifully at first.

What chemical fertilizer or manure did you use?

We used sheep manure below each plant. It was fairly well rotted.

It appears that your plants started well but then got their roots down into that manure and were burned. This would have the die-back effect on the leaves.

But I've always thought that manure was supposed to be great fertilizer for a garden.

The only way I like to see manure or chemical fertilizer used is to mix it well into the soil. Any concentration near the root system can result in burnt roots and damaged plants.

What can I do to save the plants now?

There are two steps you could take to minimize the effect of manure once it has been applied. One is a heavy irrigation with a sprinkler for sufficient time to allow the water to penetrate at least 20 cm (8 in). Repeat the sprinkling on a weekly basis if there is no heavy rain until new growth starts. This will dilute and leach down into the subsoil the fertilizer salts in the manure that are causing the trouble. The other step is to cultivate the soil between waterings to increase the air supply to the soil. This will speed up the decomposition of the manure.

When manure is used it should be incorporated well throughout the soil. The risks involved with putting manure in concentration near the root system of a plant outweigh the possible benefit. Manure should be applied with any compost during the fall preparation. In a small pile, manure freezes solid and takes longer to thaw out in the spring than soil. It might not be ready to spread when the garden is ready to dig in the spring.

Most gardeners are convinced of the benefits of manure even though they may be a little fuzzy about how and why it works. Animal and poultry manure is a scarce commodity in most parts of the country. However, gardeners convinced that it will do great things for their garden will go to great lengths to get a trailer-load of the real thing.

Manure does increase soil productivity and fertility, but the degree of benefit depends on the source and age of the manure, on how it has been stored, and on the material or absence of material used for bedding.

The actual chemical nutrient (fertilizer) content of manure varies greatly depending on which farm animal is the source.

WEIGHT OF NUTRIENTS IN .9 TONNE (1 TON)
OF ANIMAL MANURE INCLUDING BEDDING

KIND OF ANIMAL	NITROGEN kilos/pounds		PHOSPHORUS kilos/pounds		POTASH kilos/pounds	
Horse	13	29	5	11	12	26
Cow	11	24	3	7	10	22
Pig	10	22	7	15	9	20
Sheep	16	35	7	15	18	40
Steer	15	33	6	13	8	40
Hen (No bedding)	22	48	16	35	10	22
Duck	11	24	29	64	10	22

It is apparent from the table that the main benefit of manure is not its actual chemical nutrient content. Chicken droppings with no bedding have the highest nitrogen content of manures at 1 per cent nitrogen. The nitrogen in manure, unlike chemical fertilizer, is slowly soluble. This could explain why manure is particularly effective on sandy soil. Rainwater or irrigation moves quickly down through sandy soil, leaching out chemical nitrogen. This does not happen with the slow release of nitrogen in manure. Phosphorus in manure is more readily available than its chemical counterpart, potash about the same in manure and chemical fertilizer. As much as two-thirds of the chemical content of manure can be lost by improper storage. the leaching action of rain and the escape of valuable nitrogen in the form of ammonia gases.

The organisms in manure originate in the animal's digestive tract. These organisms help to break down the organic matter used as bedding and any organic matter in the soil, releasing chemical nutrients and making them available to the plant. To break down organic matter, nitrogen is required, and this is often taken from the soil and plants until the organic matter is decomposed. This is particularly true when wood shavings or sawdust are used as bedding. Soil that is fertile enough to produce vigorous growth in vegetables, indicating ample nitrogen reserve, can usually digest the organic matter in fresh manure without nitrogen starvation to the crop planted after its application. A poor soil cannot, particularly if the manure contains wood shavings.

On the other hand, the nitrogen reserves which are built up by the micro-organisms are, on decomposition, returned to the soil. In this way, micro-organisms conserve nitrogen which otherwise could be leached out by rainfall.

Fresh manure, particularly from poultry, has a greater tendency to burn root systems. Using manure liberally as the activator in a compost heap eliminates these problems. In addition, most weed seeds present in manures will be destroyed by proper composting. Frequently gardens are plagued by a particularly noxious weed whose origin can be traced back to the application of uncomposted manure.

Inorganic Fertilizers: Granular vs. Water Soluble

I know I should be fertilizing my vegetable garden but there are so many brands available that I get confused. What is the difference between granular and water-soluble fertilizers and which is more effective?

Inorganic fertilizers, sometimes called chemical, artificial or synthetic, have different attributes that increase or decrease their value. The most inexpensive form of plant nutrient is granular chemical fertilizer. The analysis printed on the container indicates the percentage by weight of the nitrogen, phosphorus and potash available. The rate at which they are available varies with each element. Usually the nitrogen is very readily soluble and is available as soon as it comes in contact with sufficient moisture to dissolve it. The phosphorus is very immobile in the soil and very slowly soluble, taking up to several months. The potash is fairly quickly available.

Plants require a steady supply of each element as they put on new growth. To make the fertilizer conform to the requirements of the plant, some manufacturers have coated the highly soluble nitrogen with sulphur, slowing down its solubility to keep pace with the plant's growth. This adds cost but makes the fertilizer much more efficient and prevents burning. In sandy soils the nitrogen cannot be leached out into the subsoil if you use a sulphur-coated, controlled-release nitrogen source. This treatment will be clearly stated on the container.

So are water-soluble fertilizers the safest bet?

Solubility in water is only a plus if the fertilizer will quickly and totally dissolve in water. Water-soluble fertilizers can vary in quality. Some, after thorough mixing even in warm water, have a residue fall-out when allowed to stand. This indicates an inferior product. It means that some element has not dissolved. You have no way of knowing which one. The mark of a good water-soluble fertilizer is total solubility so that it gives quicker results.

How do I choose the correct ratio for my garden?

The best way of choosing the correct fertilizer for your garden is to have the soil analysed (see page 17). With random applications of fertilizers over the years, soils can get out of balance, often reducing the yield and/or quality of the crop. I find that a rough rule of thumb for most small fruit and vegetable crops is to use a fertilizer with major elements in a 10-15-20 ratio. However, this is only one indicator. Soil analysis is the best indicator, and the type and quality of growth is the next. A sandy open soil, for example, generally will require more fertilizer than a clay soil due to the leaching action of rain.

Calculate the area to be fertilized and apply the maximum amount recommended on the fertilizer container, either before or after the first cultivation. A little is good; a lot is **not** better.

There is no mysterious elixir in fertilizer. It is simply a matter of mathematics. If you have a choice between one brand of water-soluble fertilizer that is 60 per cent NPK for 250 grams @ $2.00 and another that is 7 per cent NPK for 225 grams @ $2.00 then the first is far, far better value. In the first instance 60 per cent of 250 grams is 150 grams of actual plant nutrients. If we divide that into $2.00 you are paying $1.33 for 100 grams of actual plant fertilizer. In the second instance 7 per cent of 225 grams is 16 grams of actual plant fertilizer, and 100 grams of this would cost you $12.40, over nine times the cost of the first. These are actual examples taken from retail store shelves. The contrast in value was even greater than the price would indicate. In addition to the NPK in the less expensive fertilizer, the analysis also revealed that it contained minor or trace elements which are required for optimum balanced plant growth. They include iron, copper, zinc, manganese, boron, molybdenum and chlorine. Generally these occur naturally in most topsoils but adding them in trace amounts is good insurance. With the exception of chlorine, trace elements are only sold in the better grades of water-soluble fertilizer.

There is a definite advantage to applying the recommended dilution of a water-soluble fertilizer to plants, particularly at time of transplanting and shortly after. The solution will be immediately available to the plant for the expansion of roots and leaves. Water-soluble fertilizer is also an excellent way of supplying plant nutrients to potting soil in containers.

Fertilizer is also available in a controlled-release form. In this type, the manufacturer coats tiny pellets of water-soluble fertilizer with a thin plastic membrane. When the pellets come in contact with moisture, it passes through the membrane and dissolves the fertilizer which in turn is gradually released to the soil by osmotic action through the plastic membrane. For a period of three to six months, nutrients are made available to the plant without danger of burning. This form of controlled-release fertilizer can also be put on the surface of a pot or container. The fertilizer is carried down to the root system each time water is applied. A season's supply can be applied at one time.

Another form of controlled-release fertilizer are capsules or spikes. These are manufactured in such a way as to give slow yet predictable release of the major chemical elements required. Again, the risk of burning is minimal and a whole season's supply can be applied in one operation. These are excellent for fertilizing fruit trees and bushes.

Fertilizing Fruit Trees

My fruit trees are not growing. Quite a few of the leaves turn yellow and then brown during the summer. The fruit is very small.

This would appear to be lack of fertilizer. Are they planted in a lawn where the sod grows over the root system?

Yes, but we do fertilize the lawn.

The grass is likely using up the fertilizer you apply before it reaches the root system of the tree. You have two levels of plants that you must support with fertilizer: the grass and the fruit tree. This area will require more fertilizer than if it were just grass or just fruit trees. However, if you put extra fertilizer on the surface, it will overstimulate the grass and may even burn it. I would recommend that you put the fertilizer for the fruit trees down deep where it will be less available to the grass and more readily available to the deeper root system of the trees.

How can I do this?

24

There are two methods. One is to auger holes within the area of the tree's root system. This includes all the area under the tree plus 30 cm (12 in) beyond thedrip line of the widest branches. The holes should be 4 to 5 cm (1 1/2 to 2 in)in diameter and 30 to 46 cm deep (12 to 18 in) depending on the age of the tree. The holes should be 30 cm (12 in) apart on younger trees to 46 cm (18 in) apart on older trees. An electric drill with a 4 cm (1.5 in) auger-type wood bit will do the job nicely.

How much fertilizer do I put on each tree and what kind do I use?

The amount of fertilizer can be calculated by the area penetrated by the root system which is usually about 30 cm (12 in) beyond the drip line. Measure from the trunk to this point and calculate the area by squaring this dimension (the radius of the root system) and multiplying by 3.14. For example, if the radius of the root system was 2 m (6 ft) then the area would be 2 m × 2 m = 4 × 3.14 = 12.6 m² (6.5 ft × 6.5 ft = 42.3 × 3.14 = 133 ft²). The rate of application should be 227 grams of actual nitrogen fertilizer per 10 m² (8 oz of actual nitrogen fertilizer per 100 ft² of area). Fruit trees have a high nitrogen requirement and a lawn fertilizer manufactured with controlled-release sulphur-coated nitrogen is an excellent source of this. An analysis of 18-6-9 is typical of a good lawn fertilizer.

Is the second method any simpler?

It appears to be simpler but the problem is that if you apply the fertilizer at the dosage recommended by the manufacturer of the equipment, not nearly enough is applied.

The fertilizer is applied by fertilizer cartridges in the chamber of a root fertilizing device. This has a 1 m (36 in) steel wand with holes near the bottom. The wand is pushed down into the soil at about 61 cm (24 in) intervals around the drip line of the branches. A hose at the top is connected to a pressure water supply and water runs through the fertilizer chamber (slowly dissolving the fertilizer), down the wand and out the holes near the bottom. This places a dilute fertilizer solution in the root area of the tree. The manufacturer of this equipment recommends two cartridges of a 9-46-15 analysis per 3 cm (1 in) of trunk diameter, each month for five months. However, 9 per cent nitrogen of this amount works out to only 113 g (4 oz). The tree will require three times this amount for optimum growth and fruit production.

While the wand-type root fertilizing device does not meet the recommended fertilizer requirements of a fruit tree, it is an excellent device for the deep watering often required in the mid-summer.

It is important that the main bulk of the fertilizer be made available to the fruit trees in the spring and early summer when active leaf expansion and fruit development occur. The drill-and-fill method in April achieves this objective. No fertilizer should be applied from July on. Root fertilizing after July could promote soft growth, poor quality fruit and winter injury.

The formulas given to calculate fertilizer requirements appear complex at first glance, but if followed step by step they give reliable results. The formulas are essential to be able to relate tree size to nutrient needs and to be able to deal with any fertilizer analysis and come up with the right amount per tree.

With the drill-and-fill method, use a funnel which fits the hole drilled and evenly distribute the correct amount among the holes. One of the bonuses of the drilling is aeration of the soil. The holes allow the oxygen necessary for healthy roots to penetrate to the roots. This may be even more beneficial than the actual fertilizer, particularly in heavy soils.

To capitalize on the aeration potential of the holes, backfill them with mixture of half peat moss and half coarse, sharp sand, perlite, or Turface (calcide clay). This forms an almost permanent air passage to the root system. For auger holes of 3 cm (1 in) or less, backfilling is not essential.

The phosphorus content of the fertilizer does not disperse in the soil. If applied to the surface soil only, it may never reach the deep root system of the fruit tree. With the drill-and-fill wand methods, the phosphorus is placed right at the root system of the tree.

Another method of promoting vigorous growth and fruit production is to remove the sod over the entire root system of the tree to a point 30 cm (12 in) beyond the drip line. This is quite feasible on dwarf fruit trees. The fertilizer can then be applied in a band, following the drip line of the outer branches. This is the most active area of the roots (if this amount were applied to the sod in this manner it would burn the grass). The area under the tree could then be mulched with bark, cocoa bean shells or peat moss to retain moisture and give an attractive appearance.

Ingredients for a Compost Heap

I am interested in a discussion on composting. Last year I put in waste material from the garden and kitchen and threw on some soil once in a while but nothing good seemed to happen. Isn't composting just letting organic material rot?

Far from it. If you simply dump all your vegetable and fruit trimmings, egg shells, tea and coffee in a plastic bag, composter or a pile, you will soon end up with a vile-smelling, putrid mess. The art and science of composting is to bring together animal manure, lime, soil, kitchen and garden wastes, correctly combining these things in a pile with water and in the presence of air. The bacterial activity uses nitrogen and oxygen to digest the material into the humus which is so beneficial to plant growth.

What organic matter do you use?

Practically any organic plant material is eligible for compost. The wider the variety, the better the compost. We have turned oak sawdust and shavings into loamy, fertile compost in twelve weeks. Large twigs and branches can be broken down by spreading them thinly over the driveway and having the car run over them. In addition to the waste material you need nitrogen to start bacterial activity. The best source of this is reasonably fresh animal manure.

I live in the city and fresh manure is sometimes difficult to get. Is there anything else I can use?

If fresh manure is not available, the nitrogen can be obtained by applying ammonium nitrate (33-0-0), urea (46-0-0) or any high nitrogen fertilizer (e.g. 18-12-19) or a like analysis. This is frowned upon by organic gardeners but it does work well. Use approximately 450 mL (2 cups) per 1.5 m^2 (5 ft^2) layer of compost.

Do I just mix all this stuff together?

Lay down a 15 cm (6 in) layer of the coarser organic waste, then 2.5 to 5 cm (1 to 2 in) of manure, 6 mm (1/4 in) of good garden soil and enough agricultural or dolmitic limestone to grey up the soil. Moisten the layers with a hose and spreader until the layer is as moist as a squeezed-out sponge. Repeat layer after layer until the pile is at least 1 m high (39 in).

The layering should be loose and airy. Never trample the pile. Air is important. The soil provides bacteria and, combined with the limestone, neutralizes the usually acidic waste material. It is important that the lime be finely ground. The closer it is to the size of flour, the better it will work. Coarse lime has little or no effect on the acids present in soil or plant wastes. Dolmitic limestone has the added benefit of containing magnesium, a minor element required for plant nutrition.

After I've layered the compost, do I then just wait for it to turn into humus?

It's also important to turn the compost. The pile should be turned inside out to expose all the material to the heat, and incorporate more oxygen for continuing bacterial activity. Turning also gives you an opportunity to add moisture. Usually, if the pile has really "worked," it is necessary to wet it down as you turn it, again until it is as moist as a squeezed sponge. If, when you turn the compost, you find pockets of dry, ashen material, you have not had enough moisture. It may be necessary in the hot weather to put a sprinkler on an active pile for a few hours to wet it down. The heat generated and surface evaporation can consume more water than can be incorporated when the pile is made up or turned. The pile should be turned three weeks after it is made up and again five weeks after this turning.

Most failures with composting result from trying to have a running compost heap, adding the wastes as they occur. I have never been able to make this work. The key to successful composting is that the pile be made at one time. This means that the main ingredient, waste organic matter, must be stored until enough is accumulated to make up the pile.

One of the essential reactions in composting (as opposed to rotting) is the heat which occurs — up to 71° C (160° F). In my forty years' experience with composting, this seldom, if ever, occurs unless the heap is **at least** 125 cm × 125 cm × 125 cm (4 ft × 4 ft × 4 ft). Without this heat, disease and weed seeds are not destroyed and the resulting material is of dubious value. This heat is only possible if the material is first dried in the same manner and to the same degree as a farmer dries hay. **At this stage,** moisture is the enemy. Storing wet material will lead to premature decay — not composting.

Almost invariably, kitchen wastes are high in moisture content and have been further wet down in the process of cleaning the fruit and vegetables. They must be set out where they can dry. One, two or three days in the sun and air will reduce most plant material to a state that will not decompose when stored. The same principle applies to green material from the garden. If you do not have a place to do this with kitchen wastes, both dry peat moss or calcide clay (kitty litter, Turface) will sop up the moisture. They are also valuable additives to your compost.

Making Your Own Compost Box

I am interested in buying a compost bin, or making my own if it is not too expensive. What would you recommend?

A three-compartment composter is efficient and fairly easy to build. It allows you to store the compost in one end. When this is full, the compost is forked into the centre compartment and digesting begins. The third compartment can be used to store the finished compost until it is ready to be used.

How long should it take to make compost?

About twelve weeks, depending on the air temperature. The temperatures of late fall and winter in most of temperate North America preclude effective composting by lowering the compost temperature and preventing bacterial activity. The latest date to begin the compost process is about August 1st to have it completed by November 1st. After August 1st, I suggest you store the material to be processed until the weather warms up the following spring.

Can I actually store the organic wastes in the composter during the winter?

Yes. All three bins can be covered with plywood, converting them to storage of late fall and winter material. Plastic can be stapled around the composter to keep out snow.

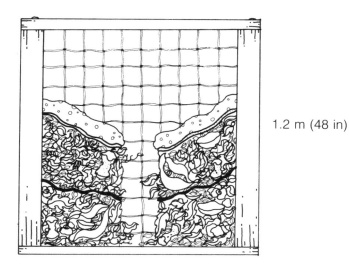

1.2 m (48 in)

Ingredients for a compost heap
Lay down a 15 cm (6 in) layer of the coarser organic waste, then 2.5 to 5 cm (1 to 2 in) of manure, 6 mm (¼ in) of garden soil mixed with limestone. Repeat this layering until the pile is at least 1 m (39 in) high.

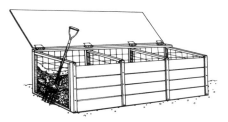

A three-compartment composter can be kept dry with a plywood cover. All three compartments can be used to store organic waste during the winter.

29

The storage pile of the three-compartment composter should be kept dry at all times. Cover this portion with a single sheet of plywood or a piece of canvas. When forking the stored material into the centre compartment, a chimney in the centre of the pile is an excellent idea because it provides a sure supply of oxygen. This can be done by standing up a 1.3 m (5 ft) length of 15 cm (6 in) stove pipe and forming the pile, layer by layer, around it. Remove the stove pipe the last thing and it will leave a well-formed air duct in the centre of the pile where it is needed. Within a few days, you should see and feel heat rising out of the centre hole. You may be shocked to feel how hot it gets. This is a sure sign that your compost is working. Reinstall the centre stove pipe before turning the compost the first time. At the final turning the stove pipe air vent is no longer necessary.

It's been my experience that if the composting is properly done it will reach a high temperature and effectively control plant disease and weeds. No sterilizing is necessary provided the temperature of 71° C (160° F) is attained. You can check this with a thermometer during composting. A properly functioning compost heap does not smell putrid; it should have a pleasant woodsy smell. It will not harbour flies or other obnoxious insects. However, it will only remain clean if carefully covered with plastic after the composting is finished.

A manufactured composter silo is available that features a rugged double-wall plastic construction to maintain heat generated by bacterial action. The Canadian design is pleasing in appearance and effective in composting.*

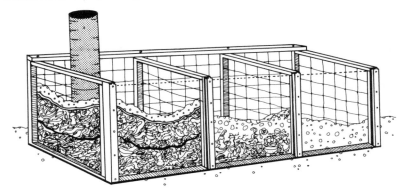

A length of stove pipe placed in the middle of the pile during the layering process will provide a necessary air vent.

*Manufacturer: B.R.M. Ltd., P.O. Box 249, Station Z, Toronto, Ontario

Chapter 2: Vegetables

Growing Asparagus

I planted asparagus seeds which have come up very nicely. How do I go about transplanting them into a proper bed?

I would let them grow all season and freeze back in the fall. Mark the exact location of the row before the fern dies back completely. In the meantime prepare the permanent site for your asparagus bed the summer before by carefully digging out all perennial weeds (dandelions, burdock, plantain) and grasses (twitch or couch). As soon as you can dig next spring, dig out the dormant asparagus roots and separate them into individual plants. Each plant will have small dormant white spear initials attached to the point where all the roots join. Any frosts that occur after the spears begin to appear may cause the root to go dormant, reducing the output of spears.

How deep should they be planted?

A commercial grower would plant them with the crown 10 to 15 cm (4 to 6 in) below grade to allow cultivating over top of the rows while they are still dormant in the spring. Placing the crown to 8 cm (3 in) below grade would allow you to do the same cultivation if you use a domestic rototiller carefully.

How far apart should the plants be in the rows and how far apart should the rows be?

In the right location asparagus will produce for twenty-five years, with the crowns covering more and more space. For the home garden, space the roots 30 cm (12 in) apart in the row and the rows 1 m (3 ft) apart.

When can I cut the asparagus?

A newly planted row should not be cut for two years after it is transplanted into the permanent site. By the third year, you can begin cutting all spears that appear when they reach a length of 15 to 20 cm (6 to 8 in). Cut everything — thin and thick spears — for a period of two to three weeks. Then allow it to grow to fern. The cutting season can be extended a week each year until the middle to the end of June is reached. Always cut above the crown but below the soil surface. A sharp V-shaped knife sometimes used for cutting out dandelion roots makes an excellent asparagus knife. Never leave cut-off stumps above the soil. They use up water and contribute nothing to growth.

It takes one to two years to grow your own asparagus roots from seed to a plantable size. Most garden centres sell roots ready to plant as soon as your garden is workable in the spring. In the fall when the fern freezes and turns brown, all the part of the plant above ground can be removed or allowed to stay and removed early the next spring.

Asparagus responds well to heavy fertilizing with both manure and chemical fertilizer; 2 kg (4 lb) of 10-15-20 fertilizer per 9 m² (100 ft²) per year is adequate but this could be applied twice on sandy soils, once when the plant is dormant and again at the end of June when the fern is allowed to develop.

Another prime requirement is well-drained sandy or light clay loam. Asparagus will not tolerate "wet feet" — a soil that does not drain quickly after thawing out in the spring or after a rainfall. It is extremely deep rooting. I once dug a well in an old asparagus bed and there were still roots the size of my little finger at a depth of 4 m (13 ft) below the surface.

Asparagus will not grow in my garden in Woodbridge. The soil is heavy clay that is slow to drain and the roots die out and disappear. In the right soil, however, it is a marvelous vegetable to grow. Freshly cut asparagus lightly cooked upright in boiling water has a flavour that is impossible to imagine until you have experienced it.

Cauliflower Turns Yellow

We've been trying to grow cauliflower this summer but are not having much luck. The heads are all turning a yellowish colour.

White cauliflower will turn an unappealing yellow in the presence of sunlight. Taking the outer leaves and tying them loosely around the head will keep out this light. The tying operation should be done when the inner leaves, the ones that curl tightly around the growing head, will no longer cover the head. If a cauliflower is tied when the head is too small, the head tends to stop growing. If it is tied too late, the head will be streaked with yellow where there are no protecting leaves.

When should I do this tying?

Once the plants are 40 to 60 cm (16 to 24 in) high they will need to be checked for head formation and the need of tying.

Do I just wind string around the whole thing, leaves and all?

Use lightweight cotton cord, holding the ball in one hand and the end of the string in the other. The string is placed around the leaves with a sweeping circular motion that lifts the leaves and puts the string near the tip. Then tie it. This will form a loose but opaque canopy around the head with room for the cauliflower to grow under its hood of leaves.

Then how will I know when they're ready to pick?

Later you can part the leaves to check size and maturity. Once the head is pressing tightly against the leaves, it's ready to cut. The other sign of maturity is a change in the curds or flower buds from a knobby cloud-like appearance to a smoother, ricey appearance. This transition can take place in a matter of days in hot weather.

Wrap the string loosely around the leaves and tie at the tip. When the head is pressing against the outer leaves, the cauliflower is ready to cut.

Cauliflower is a cool weather crop. While certain varieties will mature with reasonable quality in midsummer, the best quality is obtained with fall maturity. Early varieties should be transplanted into your garden as soon as the weather allows. However, even these varieties recommended for summer maturity will often produce a loose, ricey head when they mature in the heat. The only way to avoid this is to sow later, to mature in late August, September and October.

In June, seeds for late summer and early fall maturity can be sown in a small row in your garden, spacing the seeds about 3 cm (1 in) apart. Cover the seeds with about 1 cm (1/3 in) of soil and keep moist. Choose a full sun location and sandy soil. If you do not have this sort of soil, then hoe out a trench about 5 cm (2 in) deep and wide and fill it with sand or a mixture of half sand, half peat. This produces hardy seedlings with good root systems and helps to avoid a disease of cauliflower, cabbage, and Brussels sprouts called black leg. The disease attacks the seedling at the soil line and destroys it.

Transplant the seedlings into the permanent row about 75 cm (30 in) apart. Once transplanted, cauliflower require rich, friable soil that does not bake into a brick-like mass that is impossible to cultivate when either dry or wet. The top of the soil needs to be loosened with shallow cultivation on a weekly basis to allow air to penetrate to the roots. When watering, always apply enough to penetrate 10 to 15 cm (4 to 6 in) to encourage deep rooting. Throughout the growing season, keep a watchful eye for the light green 3 cm (1 in) cabbage worm. The control is rotenone, sevin or *Bacillus thurengiensis* dust. Any sightings of a pale yellow butterfly, the adult stage of the cabbage worm, should alert you to search out the worm. If one is enclosed inside the leaves during the tying operation, you will have a very messy cauliflower at maturity.

Any severe check in growth caused by heat, unsuitable soil, lack of cultivation or extreme heat or cold will cause cauliflower to stop growing and form a head prematurely. The plant then is dwarf and will never grow properly again. This can happen to small transplants if they are severely chilled or held too long in containers or in the garden under adverse conditions.

Cauliflower varieties recommended for fall crops will stand quite heavy frosts and recover to go on growing. A pure white cauliflower cut fresh from your garden on a crisp fall day is a satisfying achievement and a taste delight. It can be enjoyed immediately or fast-frozen for a later, midwinter treat. In addition to the white cauliflower, there are two other unique colours, purple and chartreuse. The latter two taste like cauliflower, turn an appetizing light green when cooked, but do not require tying of the leaves around the head.

Celery Not Growing

I purchased some celery plants at a nursery and planted them about two months ago. However, they simply have not grown. They are still about the same size as when I transplanted them.

What type of soil do you have?

It's hard clay. I put about 170 dm³ (6 ft³) of peat on it each year but it's not changing the clay very much. It's just like cement when it dries out.

Celery, to grow well, demands a very open soil. Generally commercial vegetable growers grow celery on mucklands, reclaimed marshes where the soil is almost pure organic matter. You can dig into it any time except winter with your bare hands. This kind of soil also supplies the other requirement for good celery, and that is adequate, consistent moisture. Both these key ingredients are missing where you are attempting to grow. The soil you have can be amended with sufficient peat moss but it would require a 10 cm (4 in) depth of peat for every 8 cm (3 in) depth of soil converted. It may be cheaper to bring in good loam for your vegetable garden.

Celery can be successfully grown in non-muck soils but the soil must be rich and readily worked. Special care must be taken with watering so that the plants never dry out. They must receive continuous moisture to avoid a stringy texture and strong flavour. Hard, dry soil will cause the plant to harden and often it will go to seed prematurely.

If our questioner had already transplanted the celery plants into rich, open loam with even moisture available, then the stunting problem likely would have originated in the nursery from overcrowding and severe wiltings.

Occasionally aphids will take up residence on celery. They can be controlled with diazinon, malathion, endosulphan or rotenone. Leaf blight which destroys the leaves can usually be controlled by the fungicide maneb.

Celery responds well to supplementary applications of 28-14-14 or 20-20-20 water-soluble fertilizer. Dilute at a rate of 14 mL per 4.5 litres (one tablespoon per gallon) using half a litre (one pint) of solution per plant, followed by a watering to take the fertilizer down to the roots.

Fruit Set in the Gourd Family

I have zucchini, vegetable marrow, and cantaloupe in my garden. They are just covered in blossoms but they have not fruited. It's as if they were all male flowers.

The vegetables giving you the problem of fruit set are all members of the gourd family of plants. Cucumber, pumpkin, watermelon and several squash are also members of the *Aucurbitaceae* (gourd) family. These vine-type plants produce the male and female parts in separate flowers. To achieve pollination and fruit set it is absolutely essential that mature pollen be taken from the anthers of the male flower and placed on the stigma of the female flower. Normally this is accomplished by the busy honeybee. But the bee population has been hurt by spreading urban communities and the ignorant use of insecticides on open blooms where bees feed. When I was a boy, the local beekeeper cooperated with us and the love life of the cucumbers by putting two or three hives of bees next to the greenhouse.

But I've seen bees around my plants.

Then the problem may be the production of unisex flowers. On certain varieties only male flowers may be produced under conditions of long summer days and high temperatures. Under low temperatures and short days the female flowers tend to predominate in certain varieties.

How can I tell whether I have male or female flowers?

The female flower which bears the fruit has an embryo similar to the shape of the final fruit between the flower and the plant stem. This embryo is absent on the male. The inner sexual parts are also quite different in shape.

How can I get fruit now if I do have both types of flower?

If indeed the weather and day length have affected the male/female ratio, then these conditions must change before the ratio alters. If, however, you can clearly discover both flower types, then with a tiny watercolour brush you can mechanically take pollen from the male and put it on the stigma of the female. Another method is to remove the male flower, trim off the petals and touch the pollen-covered anther to the stigma of the female flowers. The task will give you a deep appreciation of the work of the honeybee.

Some of the newer hybrid cucumbers, while giving fantastic yields of fruit sized to meet the needs of pickling or slicing, have also complicated the gardener's vocabulary. If you check the latest catalogues in the cucumber section, you will come across descriptive words like gynoecious and monoecious. Up until the early 1960s, most cucumber varieties were monoecious, i.e. they produced male and female flowers on the same plant. In the mid and late sixties plant breeders introduced the new gynoecious varieties, i.e. plants that bear only female flowers. With gynoecious varieties another variety bearing only male flowers (androecious) is introduced as a percentage of the total seed sown to ensure pollination. The flowering habits of the gynoecious hybrids are such that they produce many, many more blooms than the older monoecious varieties. The yield is greatly increased provided that extra fertility and moisture are provided to support the crop.

Leafy Peppers with no Fruit

We have a very large vegetable garden and everything has done well this year except for the green peppers. We have two dozen plants with beautiful thick foliage but a total harvest of only six peppers.

Peppers do best in a soil lean on nutrients, particularly nitrogen. Most other vegetables respond to a high nutrient level. The fact that everything else in your garden did well indicates a fertile soil. For the peppers another year, I would plan where you are going to plant them and do not fertilize or manure for one year.

There are a number of factors that affect yield on peppers besides soil condition. The first is the weather in late May and June when the flowers are forming. Cool days and colder nights either prevent flower bud formation or cause the buds and flowers to drop. This is a critical period in the life of peppers. It will likely do harm to set out peppers before there is some long-range prediction of night temperatures 13° C (55 ° F) and above. If you have purchased your plants from a nursery and the weather is not right then repot them from the nursery container to one plant per 10 cm (4 in) pot. Keep the plants in a warm, bright window and put them outside when the night temperatures are warm enough. Use good potting soil and water when the top 13 mm (1/2 in) of the soil is dry to the touch. Handled this way there will be no delay in the harvest date. Also keep in mind that some varieties of peppers will set fruit under cool weather conditions better than others. A reliable nursery or seed catalogue can give you information in this regard. Generally speaking, the newer hybrid varieties are more reliable in setting fruit, more abundant in yield and of a more uniform size.

Another factor is adequate pollination of the flowers. A low or non-existent bee population can dramatically affect production.

Leeks

I still have leeks growing in my garden even though it is the beginning of November. Can I store them?

Only for a limited time in the refrigerator. While leeks have a mild, onion-like flavour, they do not form a hard skin like onions which would allow you to store them.

How do you cook them?

You are talking to the wrong member of the family. My wife, Lorraine, makes a delicious leek soup. I will send you a copy of the recipe.

Leeks are delicious and a satisfying vegetable to grow. They can be grown as a transplant, sowing the seeds in late February. If you sow them carefully, spacing the seeds in the rows 1 cm (1/3 in) apart and the rows 5 cm (2 in) apart, they can be allowed to grow undisturbed until planted outdoors in mid-April. If your rows of seedlings germinate thicker than this, you can pull out and discard or transplant the extra seedlings.

Leeks, with knowledgeable encouragement, will form the long white stock that is the edible portion. This can be achieved by planting them in a 30 cm × 30 cm (12 in × 12 in) trench, the bottom half of which should be filled with compost or the richest soil of your garden. They should be planted about 15 cm (6 in) apart in this rich soil in the trench. By the time of transplanting they resemble a stem of grass. Water them with a starter solution of water-soluble 10-52-12 fertilizer.

As the leeks grow, cultivate the soil around the stems, gradually raising the level to an even grade or a little above. This cuts off the light and blanches the stem. Even moisture and fortnightly applications of 20-20-20 fertilizer will promote rapid growth and a mild flavour.

The blanching can also be achieved by adding compost to the soil before planting the leeks in rows on an even grade. Then progressively hill the soil up around the leeks as they grow.

Leeks can also be direct sown as early as your garden can be prepared in the spring, either in the trench or on grade. Sow them sparsely, covering to no more than two or three times the thickness of the seed. As soon as possible after germination, thin out until the individual plants are 15 cm (6 in) apart in the row. Whether direct sown or transplanted, you can begin harvesting and enjoying your leeks as soon as they are 3 cm (1 in) in diameter.

In milder climates they will winter over in the ground, being quite frost resistant.

LEEK SOUP

3 chopped medium-sized leeks (white part only)
1 medium onion, chopped
28 to 43 mL (2 or 3 tablespoons) butter or margarine
4 medium potatoes
1 L (4 cups) chicken stock
250 to 450 mL (1 to 2 cups) light cream or milk
1 mL(1/4 teaspoon) mace
salt and pepper
fresh watercress or chives

Stir and saute the leeks and onion in the butter for about 3 minutes. Pare and slice the potatoes very fine. Add to the onions. Add the poultry stock and simmer the vegetables covered for 15 minutes or until tender. Put the soup through a blender, fine sieve or food processor. Add cream or milk and mace, salt and pepper to taste. Serve with a sprinkle of watercress or chives. Makes about 1.8 L (8 cups).

Green Potatoes

My question is about the lowly potato. About half the potatoes we harvested this fall are partly green. I understand the green parts are poisonous and must be cut off. What causes potatoes to go green?

It is caused by the potato being either not covered at all or not covered to sufficient depth to prevent light from reaching the tuber.

But we are farmers and we know that hilling up the soil over the tubers is essential. We did this and still we have green potatoes.

How often did you hill them?

Just once. Is there any other cause of greening?

The only known cause is exposure to light. Even excessive light in storage will do it. Potatoes in a plastic bag in a store window will go green. It is possible in your case that the hilling did not put sufficient soil over the tubers to cut out all light. Light can penetrate a shallow depth of soil. Another possibility is that heavy rains washed away the hill of soil and left the potatoes with insufficient covering. Potato farmers should hill soil up around their potatoes several times during the season. Do be careful to throw away all green portions to avoid solanine poisoning.

When to Pick Rhubarb

I have a nice patch of rhubarb in the garden and I would like to freeze some, but someone told me that after the first of August you shouldn't use rhubarb. Is that true?

When a stalk of rhubarb reaches full size and is not picked it begins to get stringy. I would think that by August, the stalks would be fibrous and unpalatable.

What is the best time to pick them then?

You can begin in the spring as soon as the stalks are long enough to be used. Rhubarb is usually the first thing out of the garden in the spring. It is at its peak from then through to mid-June. From then on the plants should be left to store food and develop roots for the next year.

Rhubarb's tart, mouth-tingling taste is a true spring tonic. The plant is perennial, and will produce more heavily each year with reasonable husbandry. Pulling the stalk out of the crown can begin the second spring after planting when the stalks are at least 20 cm (8 in) long. A quick tug with a slight sideways motion does the job neatly. Our 3 m (10 ft) row has supplied rhubarb stew and pies and acted as a "stretcher" for strawberries for ten years. Easy to prepare for the freezer, it's a healthful reminder of spring all winter long. Through the process of cloning, there has been a great improvement in rhubarb varieties. Canada Red is a new selection which retains its deep red colour the length of the stalk — even the inside is red. Check with a reliable nursery for their variety recommendation in your area.

Spinach Goes to Seed

I put spinach seeds in my garden about the 24th of May but they grew straight up with the leaves far apart.

I believe you are describing spinach going to seed. Spinach only grows vegetatively, producing the leaves that are eaten, in the cool weather of spring and fall. A combination of long days and warm temperatures causes it to bolt, or initiate seed stalks. Spinach should be one of the first vegetables sown, just as early as the frost is out and the garden can be prepared.

Will it tolerate frost after it germinates?

Definitely. As a matter of fact the rate of germination drops dramatically once the soil temperature gets above 16° C (60° F). It can also be sown in the late fall (mid-September in Southern Ontario) to winter over, producing an early vegetable the next spring. Snow cover is required to succeed with winter spinach. Grown this way, it can be cut a few leaves at a time, allowing some to remain. It will go on producing leaves as long as the spring temperatures remain cool.

Lettuce, cauliflower and broccoli also go to seed prematurely in Southern Ontario if they are matured during the hot summer months. They need to be planted very early in April or in late June to mature in the cool fall weather.

Another vegetable sold under the common name of New Zealand spinach is a member of another family of plants: *Tetragonia expanso.* Its nut-like seeds are sown early in the spring. The hard seed cover can inhibit germination unless one side of seed is rubbed on emery paper and soaked overnight in water before sowing. The seeds of New Zealand spinach can be started indoors at the same time as cabbage or cauliflower, then transplanted and set outdoors in May. The growth habit is luxurious but upright, much as our questioner described. Six or eight plants spaced about 41 cm (16 in) apart in the garden supplies a near-spinach flavoured green during the hot weather when true spinach will not perform.

Pinch out (and eat) the top 10 cm (4 in) of the plants as soon as they reach about 41 cm (16 in) to encourage bottom leaf expansion. Begin harvesting the leaves from the bottom up soon after this. Only the leaves are harvested and are used in salads or as a boiled green vegetable.

Pruning and Staking Tomatoes

I've heard that I'll get a better tomato crop if I prune my tomato plants. Is this true? I'd rather not bother with pruning if I can avoid it.

To be of benefit, pruning tomatoes has to be combined with staking or stringing the plant into vertical growth. The idea is to confine the plant to one central stem and to prune out, while they are small, all

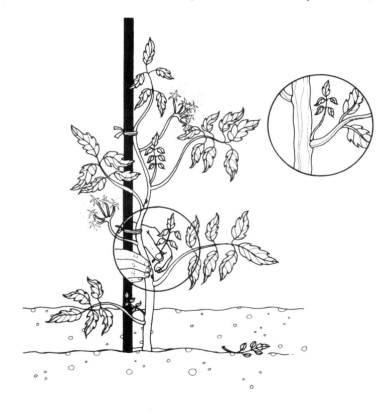

Suckers must be removed from the point where the leaf petiole joins the stem.

the lateral branches. At the same time, the stem is securely but loosely tied to the stake with a twist tie. At least one branch will form at the point where the stem of the leaf (petiole) joins the main trunk (leaf axil). Without pruning, these suckers or branches become as large as the central stem, forming a bush plant. Bush plants take a lot more ground space than a single-stem tomato grown vertically. If you have a small garden or are growing tomatoes on a patio or apartment balcony, staking and pruning have definite advantages.

Will I get as much fruit from a staked and pruned tomato plant as from one allowed to grow naturally?

No, you will not. The results of any controlled experiments that I have seen indicate that field-grown staked tomatoes yield about half of natural grown bush tomatoes. However, they yield this on one third of the space. I recommend 100 cm × 100 cm (39 in × 39 in) spacing for natural grown bush tomatoes and 61 cm × 61 cm (24 in × 24 in) for staked and pruned tomatoes. This means you can grow three staked tomatoes vertically in the same space as one natural tomato. The yield then of the staked tomatoes per square metre would be about 40 to 50 per cent higher.

But I would have to buy more plants, plus the work of pruning and tieing them up.

Correct. This is why there are fewer and fewer staked and pruned tomatoes grown commercially where they have to pay for that labour. However, often with the home gardener it's those first tomatoes from the garden that are such a treat. Although pruning does not really affect the earliness of ripening, because you can put more pruned and staked tomato plants in the space available you will get a higher yield of tomatoes at the first picking.

Are there any other advantages to pruning and staking?

Yes. The fruit is all held high off the ground. This usually results in less soft rot and slug damage than is often experienced when the fruit of natural grown tomatoes lie on the ground. However, the sprawling vines of bush tomatoes act as mulch over the ground, conserving moisture and ensuring a more even supply. With staked tomatoes, the ground is exposed and water evaporates from the soil much more quickly. This can cause uneven moisture supply, wilting and a higher incidence of blossom end rot in pruned and staked tomatoes. A mulch of plastic, cocoabean shells, peat moss or straw will conserve moisture and overcome this tendency. The staked plant also has a smaller root system.

What about the quality of the fruit?

All my experience indicates that you will get much larger tomatoes for any variety pruned and staked rather than naturally grown. If you like big tomatoes, staking is one way of achieving them. Colour and flavour seem to be the same. You will likely experience more growth cracks on staked tomatoes probably related to uneven moisture supply. Harvesting of staked tomatoes is much easier with the fruit borne high.

There is one compromise option that lies between staking and natural growing of tomatoes. That is growing in tomato cages. The wire for this is made by Stelco and is widely distributed through nurseries and hardware stores. It is a galvanized welded wire fabric sold in

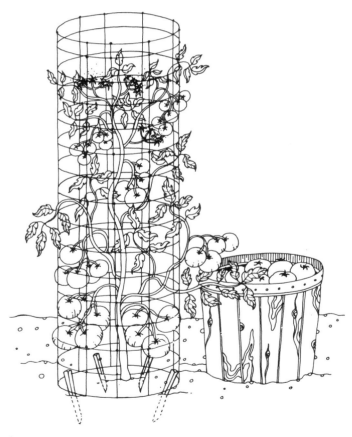

Tomato cages
Anchor the cage by driving tent pegs to anchor the bottom wire.

8 m (25 ft) rolls. You can easily make six circular cages 1 m (39 in) high and 38 cm (15 in) in diameter. The cage is placed around each plant at planting or shortly after. Wandering stems that poke out through the mesh are put back in by hand. Essentially, they are grown unpruned but should they begin to crowd, then the branches that come out through the wire can be cut off. The result is a worthy compromise between natural sprawl and labour intensive pruning and staking.

One word of caution with cages. My garden is exposed to wind and I had trouble with tomato cages blowing over in August with their load of fruit and plants. If wind could be a problem in your garden, then anchor the cage by driving tent pegs to anchor the bottom wire of the cage.

With staking, I find the simplest method of support is to use 1.9 cm × 1.9 cm (3/4 in × 3/4 in) stakes 2 m (6 ft) long. The tomatoes are planted in 60 cm × 60 cm (24 in × 24 in) space, then the stakes are driven about 15 cm (6 in) into the ground about 5 cm (2 in) from each plant and sloped inward until four stakes cross near the top like a teepee. These must be securely wired together near the top. This forms a strong self-supporting unit that will readily resist wind and carry the load of fruit.

Poor Fruit Set on Tomatoes

The blossoms on my tomato plants are falling off before the fruit sets. The crop is very poor.

Fruit on tomatoes is borne in clusters called trusses. Is the same thing occurring on each truss of flowers as they appear?

More or less. It's worse on some clusters but seems to be occurring on all of them to some degree.

Then probably you have a combination of factors at work. Flowers on tomato plants will form under a wide range of conditions. But fruit set only occurs under certain conditions. It is, for example, adversely affected by soil that is low in nitrogen. This results in stunted growth, lack of colour in the leaves and poor fruit set.

My plants are anything but stunted. They are huge and lush with big dark green leaves.

Then you must have an abundant supply of nitrogen; this is another condition that causes premature flower drop. To get maximum fruit set, the nitrogen supply must be adequate — neither high nor low. I would recommend you confirm the nitrogen levels of the soil with a soil test.

How can nitrogen be lowered if it is high?

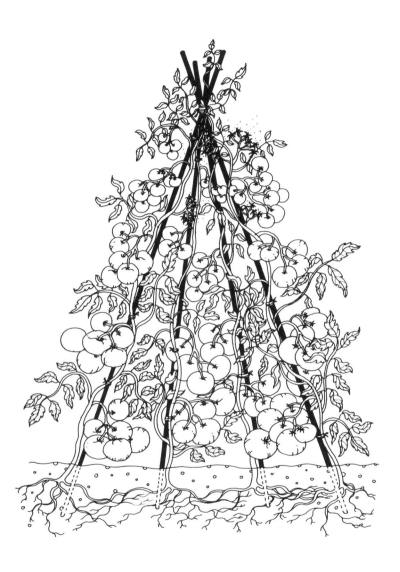

The teepee method of staking tomatoes gives three or four plants strong
support.

Spring and fall rains have a leaching effect, washing some of it down into the subsoil, especially on sandy soils. Plants use it as well, of course. The other thing to do is stop applying it to the soil. Use peat moss instead of manure for organic matter and use chemical fertilizer containing no nitrogen for at least one year. Then retest the soil. Use a fertilizer containing no nitrogen. The first number of the analysis on the bag should be zero.

If nitrogen is the problem, how come the unfruitfulness is not more uniform?

The other factor that influences fruit set is temperature. Controlled experiments show that the optimum temperature range for fruit set on tomatoes is 15° to 20° C (59° to 68° F). Below 11° C (54° F), fruit fails to set on most varieties.

We have had some cool spells. Is there anything that can be done about this?

The claim is made that some varieties will set fruit under adversely cool weather. Coldset, Springset, Scotia and Sub-Arctic Maxi are four such varieties. Certain chemicals can also help fruit set under adverse weather conditions. The generic chemicals parachlorophenoxyacetic acid (CLPA), beta-napthoxyacetic acid (NOA) and ortho-dhlorophenoxypropionic acid (CLPP) are used, but these are only beneficial if sprayed on the blossoms on a weekly basis when the weather is dropping below 15° C (59° F).

Off-Vine Ripening of Tomatoes

There is always a lot of fruit on the vines of my tomato plants when frost comes in the fall. Will this fruit ripen if I pick it before the frost?

Yes, provided you follow a few simple principles. Tomatoes cannot be conditioned to take frost. Indeed, the weather prior to the first frost will determine whether or not your tomatoes will ripen off the vine. If the day or night temperatures drop too low during the two weeks prior to frost, it will have a chilling effect on the fruit, preventing it from ripening no matter how carefully it is handled. Therefore, carefully watch weather forecasts. If the temperature begins to dip below 10° C (50° F), then begin final harvesting.

Do I pick everything on the vines?

Tomatoes go from green through whitish green, then pink and finally red-ripe. Fruit should be selected on the basis of colour rather than size. A large fruit may still be at the immature green stage and, if it ripens at all, it will not have the best colour, flavour and texture. However, fruit picked at the yellow-red stage ripened at 24° C

(75° F), in the dark, will have normal flavour and ascorbic acid.

How immature can the fruit be and still ripen?

It should be at the mature, bright, waxy green stage without showing signs of whitening, the first stage of ripening. It will not have the flavour of a tomato picked at the yellow-red stage but it will be superior to imports. Mature green is difficult to judge. If the weather indicates that the end of the growing season is near, then a few errors in judgment are better than frozen tomatoes.

Is the ideal temperature for ripening then 24° C (75° F)?

That is the optimum temperature for rapid ripening but they will ripen in temperatures ranging from 12° C (54° F) to 27° C (80° F). Above 28° C (82° F) tomatoes ripen rapidly but lack colour and flavour. The lower the temperature, the slower the ripening process. If you wish to keep the tomatoes even longer, then refrigerate them when they are at the firm, ripe stage.

Do they have to receive sunlight to ripen?

No. Light is not necessary and direct sunlight may even cause dehydration of the fruit. High humidity, around 80 to 90 per cent, is also important to prevent dehydration. The practice of covering the fruit with dry newspaper also can have an adverse dehydrating effect. Cover the ripening fruit with moistened newspapers or cheesecloth, or put a humidifier in the room. This will add to the final quality of the fruit.

Zucchini on the Rocks

I am attempting to grow zucchini up north where the season is shorter and the weather cooler. We are on rock with little or no soil so I planted my zucchini in compost in a tire on the rocks. They grew well and formed fruit, but when the fruit was 10 cm (4 in) long, the ends went soft and the squash rotted. It was so disappointing.

If you observe a zucchini carefully, you will notice that it has a male flower on a fairly long stem and a female flower attached to the plant by the embryo fruit (ovary). When the female is pollinated by bees with pollen from the male, the fruit begins to swell and lengthen and the flower, still attached to the fruit, begins to die. It's at this point that the flower is most vulnerable to attack by fungus, probably botrytis. This causes the flower to rot as well as die. The rot subsequently enters the fruit at the flower end causing it to rot. Your night temperatures would be in the 10° C range (50° F) which is an ideal condition for botrytis.

Is there any way I can control this?

Yes. Try removing the flower just after the fruit begins to enlarge. This will minimize the chance of infection. If you still have rot occuring, you will have to spray with captan, benomyl or maneb on a fortnightly basis as soon as flowers begin to appear.

The use of a tire to accelerate maturity during cool weather is well grounded in research. When the tire is placed around warmth-loving plants like tomato, cucumber, eggplant, pepper and melon, it acts as a heat collector during the day and releases heat to the plant at night. Tests were made of various ways to moderate soil temperature during the cool cloudy weather experienced in the northwest United States, and the tire proved the most effective. If the weather is consistently above 15° C (59° F) and sunny, the tire will have little effect in accelerating harvest time. It only works under adverse conditions, bringing heat-loving crops to maturity as much as two weeks earlier than un-tired check plants.

Late Vegetables

For various reasons, I have never been able to plant a vegetable garden until the beginning of July. Is there anything I can grow which will mature before frost?

Yes, there are quite a few, such as beets, broccoli, lettuce and spinach. Fairly precise spacing is required on cauliflower (75 cm or 30 in), cabbage and broccoli (60 cm or 24 in), Chinese cabbage and head lettuce (40 cm or 16 in), and leaf lettuce (20 cm or 8 in). If you are running late on these items, I would sow them at this spacing rather than sowing in a row and transplanting. Sow three seeds per space and then thin to one plant after germination. This will pick up a week to ten days on growth time.

LAST SOWING DATES FOR LATE VEGETABLES (dates are for Southern Ontario)

Bush beans: July 15 to August 1st
Beets: July 15th to August 1st
Broccoli: July 1st to 15th
Cabbage: July 1st to 15th
Chinese cabbage: July 1st to 7th
Carrots: July 1st to 15th
Cauliflower: July 1st to 15th
Swiss chard: July 15th

Sweet corn: July 1st to 15th
Head lettuce: July 7th to 20th
Leaf lettuce: August 1st to 7th
Okra: July 1st to 7th
Bunching onions: August 1st to 7th
Radishes: September 1st
Spinach: September 15th
Summer turnips: August 1st

Chapter 3: Fruit Trees

Pollination of Fruit Trees

I have just moved into a new home and have discovered that there are two plum trees in the back yard. How can I tell if they are male and female so that I can be sure I get fruit?

Some species of plants such as cucumber and zucchini squash bear some flowers with only female parts, other flowers with only male parts. Fruit trees have both male and female parts in the same flower but some kinds require cross-pollination from a different variety of the same fruit to set a good crop. The different variety can be in a neighbour's yard, but obviously the closer the tree, the more likely pollination will occur.

How can I tell which variety of plum tree I have?

Plums are more complicated than most fruit trees because there are two basic strains or types: European and Japanese. The varieties of one type will not cross-pollinate with the other and will only cross-pollinate with certain varieties of their own type. I believe your best course of action at this point is to wait and see if indeed you get fruit set. If you do not, then plant two trees of either European or Japanese that are compatible pollinators. These may also work as pollinators for the two you have. Another option is to graft European or Japanese varieties on to your present trees (see pages 64 to 71).

PLUMS

Of the European type, California Blue, Iroquois, Stanley and Damson are self-fruitful but nevertheless will benefit from cross-pollination with a compatible variety. Bluefre is partially self-fruitful but will also benefit from cross-pollination.

The most popular Japanese varieties of plums grown in Ontario (Burbank, Early Golden and Shero) are not self-pollinators. Normally the European varieties bloom much later than the Japanese and are not suitable pollinators.

APPLES

To get an optimum yield, apples require cross-pollination with another variety that blooms at or near the same time. The varieties should be within 30 m (100 ft) of each other.

Courtland is a very useful pollenizer because it is a mid-season

and long-blooming tree. Quinte and Northern Spy are poor pollen-
izers because their blooming periods do not overlap.

APRICOT

All varieties presently sold through nurseries are self-fruitful,and do
not require two varieties to pollinate.

PEAR

Consider pears as self-unfruitful requiring any two varieties to cross-
pollinate except Kieffer which is not a good pollenizer. Any two of
Bosc, Bartlett or Anjou are compatible.

SWEET CHERRY

All varieties are self-unfruitful and require another compatible variety
to cross-pollinate. Of the three most popular varieties Hedelfingen
and Vic are incompatible and should not be planted without Bing
which will pollenize either or both.

SOUR CHERRY

Varieties are all self-fruitful and any one variety may be planted alone
or in multiple planting.

PEACH AND NECTARINE

All varieties are self-fruitful and may be planted alone or in multiple
planting.

The main pollination agent for fruit trees is the honey bee. Without
an adequate number of bees, moderate weather and wind, pollination and fruit set will be adversely affected. Many urban and
suburban areas have an inadequate honey bee population. In this
case, hand pollination can be accomplished by taking mature pollen
from one variety and moving it to another compatible variety. This
is an alternative where cross-pollination is required. If the variety is
self-fruitful, mature pollen from the anthers of the bloom is placed
on the stigma of the same bloom. A tiny paint brush will do the job.

Moving Fruit Trees

I would like to transplant some cherry, peach and pear trees. When is the best time to do this?

My preference would be *early* spring in soil that becomes workable just after the frost is out. The problem often in spring planting is that the job is left too late because of bad weather or wet, unworkable soil. Then the trees are no longer dormant and suffer when planted. I believe the trees are best left undisturbed over the winter but if there is any doubt about being able to do the job quickly after frost is out in the spring, then late fall when the trees have gone dormant and dropped most of their leaves is better than late spring when the leaf buds have begun to swell or crack open. How old are these trees?

They are about three years old.

How thick are the trunks about 30 cm (12 in) up from the ground and how large are the heads?

The trunks are about 3 cm (1 in) and the heads about 60 cm (24 in).

Have you ever root pruned them?

No, how do you do that?

Root pruning does for the roots what pruning does for the branches. It causes them to branch out. This makes for a compact, fibrous root system close to the trunk that serves the tree well when it is moved. If you are in sandy soil you tend to get a more fibrous root system anyway, but if the soil is clay loam or clay then root pruning is more important. It is done on trees the size you have by taking a sharp spade and stomping it into the soil the full depth of the spade at a radius of 25 to 30 cm (10 to 12 in) from the trunk. If you can allow them to remain in their present location for another summer this procedure would take some of the risk out of moving them. If you feel you must move them now, then instead of root pruning, dig the tree out with a 60 cm (24 in) diameter of roots. If you can keep some of the soil with the roots, this will disturb them less than total soil removal.

Buying Fruit Trees

As a young girl I remember having two large cherry trees in the yard which all the kids loved for their cherries. I'd like to plant one in my backyard, but I don't really know how to go about buying a tree.

Fruit trees are sold either as whips — single-stemmed or non-branched trees about 1 1/2 to 2 m (4 to 6 ft) high — or as two-year old branched trees. The branched trees are sold by calipre, the thickness of the trunk when measured 30 cm (12 in) from the ground. The calipre is an indication of vigour and usually relates to the spread and number of branches — the larger the calipre, the larger the head size.

By a non-branched tree do you mean it just has one bare stem and no other branches?

Not exactly. It just means that there is one central stem, but there may be smaller branches near the base.

Which type is a better buy?

I think you can expect to pay more but get fruit sooner from a two-year old 3 cm (1 in) calipre tree than a lesser calipre or one-year old whip. If you do your shopping before mid-April, fruit tree whips or branched two-year old specimens may be purchased dormant and bare root (all soil removed from the roots). The root system should be examined and any broken pieces cut off.

Once you have purchased any fruit tree you have to treat it with care if you want it to produce succulent fruit. If you have purchased a whip, the central stem should be cut off 80 cm (31 in) to 1 m (39 in) from the base of the tree to encourage branching.

While this simple topping works fine on most fruit tree whips, a cherry tree whip will require further pruning to obtain branches at the right place and the right angle. Usually there are no wide-angle branches at suitable heights to form the main framework, so all branches should be removed. You will note buds all up the remaining stem. The prospective branches should be selected at 12, 3, 6 and 9 o'clock around the stem and 15 cm (6 in) apart to properly distribute the ultimate weight of fruit. When the buds are just ready to burst, mark the 4 sets of buds that are in the correct position with masking tape or clothes pins. Flick off with a knife point all the remaining buds, leaving three at each point marked. By leaving three buds, the final branches will be at an acceptable broad angle to the trunk. The following spring, prune off two of the three, leaving a sound beginning for a trained, well-shaped cherry tree.

Most people really don't get down to gardening until they can do

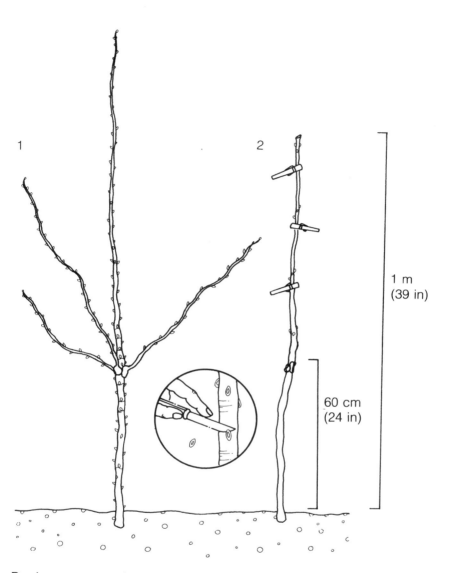

1

2

1 m
(39 in)

60 cm
(24 in)

Pruning a one-year cherry whip
1. A one-year old cherry whip after purchase. The branches are at too sharp an angle and should be pruned off.
2. First, cut the central stem off 80 cm to 1 m (31 to 39 in) from the base of the tree to encourage branching. Remove all branches. Choose four sets of three buds at 12, 3, 6 and 9 o'clock around the trunk, each set 15 cm (6 in) apart beginning at 60 cm (24 in) from the grade to the top of the whip. Flick the rest of the buds off with the point of a knife. The following spring, choose the best-positioned branch out of each set of three and prune the rest off.

it in their shirt sleeves. By this time trees are leafing out and difficult, if not impossible,to plant without fatal shock. For this reason most nurseries offer fruit trees planted in containers. There is less risk involved when you purchase a tree that is already leafed out and growing in a container as opposed to buying a dormant tree. Fruit trees are deciduous, which means they drop their leaves in the fall in response to cooler weather and shorter day length. Growth processes stop and the tree goes dormant. At this point, those destined for the market are dug, the soil shaken from the roots and the tree is stored. The storage is kept near freezing temperature to prevent growth and close to 100 per cent relative humidity to prevent drying out.

In the spring the trees are taken from storage to the retail outlet. There is always the possibility that with the shock of digging, storing, transporting and retailing, the tree will not have enough vigour to break dormancy, leaf out and grow. If you plant a bare root dormant tree and it fails to grow you have lost a year. This risk is largely eliminated when you choose a tree leafed out and growing in a container. These can be moved into your garden any time.

Pruning Young Fruit Trees

I've heard your discussions on pruning older fruit trees but I'm not sure how to tackle my young pear tree.

How old is the tree?

Well, I planted it last year but it was a fair size when I bought it. I'd say about 2 m (6 ft) high.

What you have is probably a single stemmed tree or a whip which you should have pruned at planting.

I cut off about half the tree just after I planted it. Was that the right thing to do?

The correct height to top a fruit tree whip is 80 cm to 1 m (30 to 40 in). Now you have to prune again choosing the branches that will form the main framework of the tree. Do you have some branches as a result of the top pruning you did last year?

Yes, there are several.

Pruning induces new shoot growth so you will likely find two or three new branches just below the point where you topped off the whip. All but one of these should be removed if they are crowding the main stem at sharp angles. This becomes the central leader branch. Below this select four to six main branches about 10 to 15 cm (4 to 6 in) apart up the trunk and well distributed around the trunk to keep as fruit-bearing branches. Be more concerned about the placement of these branches than the size. Pruning off all other branches will quickly result in a surge of growth in a small branch.

The top central leader branch that you have left should be cut back by one third and the rest of the longest branches should be cut back by one third to one half.

The training of a two-year old tree, whether it's a year after you have planted a whip, or a two-year old purchased dormant as a bare root or in a container grown at a nursery, is critical. It will set the fruit-bearing structure of the tree and influence its productivity and life span.

The pruning technique varies somewhat with species of fruit tree but dwarf apple, plum and cherry can be pruned the same way as the dwarf pear described.

Peach and apricot require severe pruning at the time of planting to survive. A one-year old tree will produce a lot of lateral branches which need to be pruned back to almost a whip stage. Even the

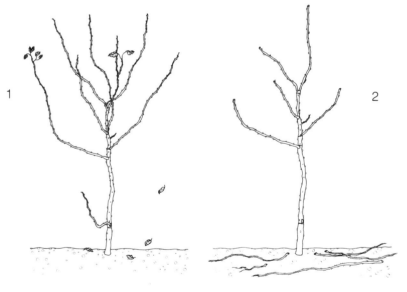

Pruning a two-year old tree
1. The tree may have been bought as a whip and topped or purchased as a two-year old tree.
2. Choose four main branches evenly spaced up the trunk and well distributed around the trunk. Choose a central leader branch (two or three new branches will likely have grown just below the point where the whip was topped off) and remove the others. Prune the leader branch by one-third; the rest of the remaining branches back by one-half.

purchase of a two-year old with bare roots will need almost as severe a pruning.

With a two-year old peach or apricot tree, you should select a terminal (uppermost) branch and cut it about 105 cm (42 in) above the ground. If there are not 5 branches spaced at about 15 cm (6 in) up the trunk and well distributed around the trunk, an extra two lateral branches may be left on the terminal branch. Remove all the rest of the lateral branches. Cut the remaining branches back to six buds, leaving stubs of about 8 to 20 cm (3 to 8 in) long. Peach and apricot trees have an inherent tendency not shared by other fruit trees to produce a lot of branches. To prevent this happening all buds and branches below the last main fruit-bearing branch should be removed. This sets the height of the lowest fruit-bearing branch at about 60 cm (24 in) above the ground.

In June examine the tree and remove all dead stubs with cuts made tight to the trunk. That's it until the following spring.

At that time select four branches of about equal size with wide crotch angles, evenly distributed around the trunk and about 15 to 20 cm (4 to 6 in) apart up the trunk. If some of the branches selected are longer than the others, they can actually be dwarfed or brought into uniformity by pruning off the least desirable laterals (those going straight up, straight down, or simply weak and spindly). This reduces the leaf area and therefore the growth rate of that branch. Prune away all secondary branches which have a 30° angle or less. These sharp angles will result in breakage, winter injury and cankers if they are not removed.

Pruning Fruit-Bearing Trees

How do I go about cutting the right branches off an apple tree in the backyard of my new home? The neighbours say that it bears fruit and I want to keep it that way.

What shape is the tree in?

Well, the branches are mostly horizontal. That's the way they're supposed to be, isn't it?

Yes, I would say that you have a tree in good condition. But you will have to go through another season so you can observe how the branches produce. Apple and pear trees bear fruit on two-year old terminal buds or short spurs along the branches. These will remain productive for several years so you wouldn't want to cut them off. If you notice that a branch is unproductive or bears fruit of uneven size and colour, determine the cause. Is the fruit on the poor branch being shaded from light? Are there unproductive branches using up light space? Note these factors during each growing season and adjust the growth with next year's pruning.

Do I cut off all the branches I think are unproductive?

A good guide to pruning is that not less than 5 per cent and not more than 10 per cent of the bearing wood be pruned out each year.

Pruning encourages the growth of branches that are in the correct position and angle on the trunk to be able to support the weight of the fruit. Branches that are at a sharp angle to the trunk cannot slough off and replace old bark as they should. The bark is trapped between the trunk and the branch, preventing the proper growth of weight-supporting wood. Pruning also distributes the fruit to receive the maximum amount of light to give size, colour and flavour, and it makes harvesting convenient. Light yearly pruning just before the leaves appear is much better than heavy pruning every three or four years. Heavy pruning encourages a heavy growth response that upsets the balance of growth to fruitfulness and thereby reduces the productivity.

PLUM

The plum bears most of its fruit on vigorous horizontal spurs on wood from two to eight years old. Plums tend to overbear. To obtain good fruit size, it is necessary to prune the bearing wood at least 10 per cent each year to induce new growth. Prune new growth to a length of about 40 cm (16 in) on young trees and about 25 cm (10 in) on older trees.

APRICOT

The apricot produces most of its fruit on short-lived spurs. Pruning should maintain a sufficient number of strong spurs to bear a good crop but induce enough new growth to produce spurs for future crop. In general it will need somewhat heavier pruning than the plum. Apricot branches tend to become long and willowy without frequent cutting back.

CHERRY

Cherries, both sweet and sour, develop most of their fruit on two and three year old wood. Seldom do the spurs produce for longer than three years. Weak wood which bears small, poorly coloured fruit should be removed each year. This usually means removal of

5 to 10 per cent of the bearing wood. For good production, prune to maintain terminal fruiting branches of 30 cm (12 in) or more where fruit spurs develop.

PEACH

Unlike apple and pear, the peach does not have a spur system of bearing fruit but relies on fruit bud development on new growth each year. It is essential to promote the health of the tree so that new growth is present to bear fruit each year. With the peach, probably 10 to 20 per cent of last year's bearing wood needs removal each year.

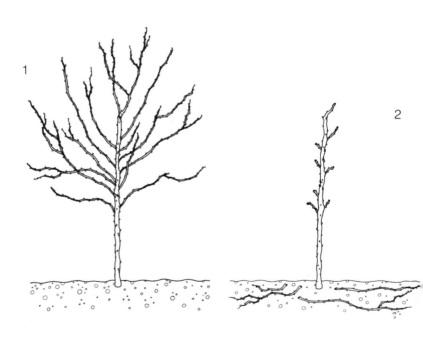

Pruning a peach tree
1. A nursery peach tree after purchase.
2. Reduce the tree to almost a whip, pruning it down to 122 cm (48 in) in height. Remove all weak and narrow-angled branches and cut all other branches to two buds.

Pruning Rules in Brief

If you follow these general rules you should have a well-proportioned tree with a good fruit yield.

1. Prune all crippled branches
2. Where two branches are growing close together, remove the least desirable, bearing in mind spacing and exposure to light.
3. Remove branches that go straight up or straight down, leaving those with a horizontal orientation.
4. Experience and observation are your best teacher. Remember that you are attempting to give each branch its place in the sun.
5. Make close, clean cuts. Avoid stubs which encourage the entry of disease and often preclude healing of the bark.
6. Prune yearly in the spring just before leaves appear.
7. Pruning stimulates new growth and can be used to encourage growth in a certain area.
8. There must be a reason for removing a branch as outlined above, otherwise leave it be. Branches bear leaves which manufacture food, maintain growth and make fruiting possible.

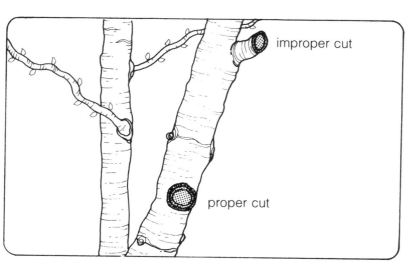

improper cut

proper cut

Proper pruning techniques
A proper cut removes the branch tight to the trunk or branch. Improper pruning leaves a stub to encourage sucker growth or die.

Grafting Fruit Trees

I have in my garden what must be a very old variety of apple. The tree could be upwards of eighty years old. The apples have a unique, mild flavour resembling a banana. They mature in mid-October and we have had no difficulty storing them until Christmas. I believe it's called Pumpkin Sweet. Can I start a new tree from seed?

Yes, but apples do not usually come true to type from seed. There can be great variations in colour, size, production and maturity. This is one reason nurseries usually propagate fruit trees by grafting.

Could a tree of this age be grafted?

Yes, grafting is as old as nature itself where roots or branches that crossed eventually formed an actual union. People have been grafting plants for centuries.

We tried rooting a stem by air layering but had no success.

Where it has become common practice to reproduce plants by grafting, it is often because they are very reluctant to propagate by air layering with cuttings off the tree in cutting beds.

Grafting is a method of plant multiplication (propagation) where living tissues from two different but compatible plants are brought together in an environment where they join and continue to grow as one. There is evidence that the Chinese practised grafting as early as 1000 B.C. The apostle Paul spoke knowledgeably about grafting in the Bible (Romans 11:17-24) where he refers to the grafting of the "good" and the "wild" olive tree. With fruit trees, it was the "wild" aspects of their character, their inability to reproduce true to type from seed, and their reluctance to root plant parts that necessitated reproduction by grafting and the resultant "good" that has come from it. Scientists have now developed rootstocks that dwarf the growth of apples, for example. At the same time these rootstocks can cause earlier maturity and larger fruit with better colour. Because of the years of painstaking research which led to the grafting "marriage" of root system to top growth, you can prune, spray and pick full-size top quality apples in your own yard without ever using a ladder.

Our questioner could take advantage of present-day knowledge of dwarfing rootstocks by grafting a part of the old Pumpkin Sweet variety on to dwarfing rootstock. The result should be the same apple conveniently growing on a tree that can be tended while standing on the ground.

Choosing Understock (Rootstock)

I'm calling from Ottawa. I want to graft an old apple tree to a young one, but I found out that there are lots of different rootstocks to choose from. How do I pick the right one?

It is essential to choose a good understock in order to produce a healthy tree and fruit. I would suggest you purchase the Robusta 5 understock which is extremely hardy in areas as cold or colder than Ottawa where winters are unbroken by mild spells of thawing.

Whether you are buying a grafted fruit tree at a nursery or are embarking (no pun intended) on a grafting project, a knowledge of understocks is invaluable. The understock will determine the size of your fruit tree, its cropping ability, its hardiness to cold and will influence the time of maturity, size and colour of the fruit.

APPLE UNDERSTOCK

The best known apple understocks were selected from a collection of European stock at the East Malling Research Station in England in the early part of this century. These selections were propagated by rooting plant parts by various means. The new plant was exactly like the original because it came from a part of the original and therefore is a true clone. Because of their overall merits observed over the years, three clonal understocks are mainly used in the milder parts of Canada.

The one that has the most dwarfing effect is M (Malling) 9. A twenty-year old McIntosh apple on M9 at the Horticultural Research Institute in Vineland, Ontario, measures 2.7 m high × 3.6 m wide (9 ft × 12 ft). Dwarf trees on M9 rootstock come into bearing quickly producing well-coloured fruit of excellent quality that can be picked from the ground. The disadvantage of M9 grafted apple trees is the brittle nature of the roots and the somewhat droopy habit of the branches. Some form of support on either posts or post-supported wires is usually necessary to prevent the tree from snapping off the root system under its fruit load and high wind.

M26 (sometimes referred to as EM26) is a fairly new virus-free dwarfing rootstock. It produces a slightly larger tree than M9. M26 will grow in heavy clay soils and the root system is not as brittle as M9. Fruit bearing begins the third year but the tree does not reach full yield potential until the ninth or tenth year. Support is normally not needed.

MM106 provides a well-anchored root system with outstanding productivity. If you have space for a more vigorous semi-dwarf tree and do not mind some ladder work to tend your trees, MM106 will yield above-average crops.

One disadvantage of all the Malling rootstocks is their lack of winter hardiness in the colder parts of Canada. The most tender part of fruit trees (and indeed most trees) is the root system. Open cultivation, coarse, textured soils and lack of snow cover can result in root injury which soon results in corresponding die-back of the top of the tree. Where you are in a borderline climatic locality, a mulch of dry straw over the root system of dwarf fruit trees can be a good tactic against winter injury.

APRICOT UNDERSTOCK

Dwarfing is not as vital an issue with apricots as the trees are inherently smaller. The most satisfactory rootstocks for growing in the fruitbelts of Ontario are Morden 604 and Veecot.

CHERRY UNDERSTOCK

Plants grown from the seed of *Prunus Mahaleb* and *Prunus avium Mazzard* are the most commonly used understock where cherries are grown, Mahaleb being the most hardy. There are no dwarfing understocks offered commercially but Montmorency, a tart cherry variety, is generally dwarfed on *Prunus fruiticosa,* an ornamental tree. This makes a dwarf, shrub-like tree about 1.5 m (5 ft) high, ideal for the home gardens.

PEACH UNDERSTOCK

Seedlings from the pits of the Alberta, Halford and Veteran peach varieties are a satisfactory understock for peaches and nectarines. As yet there is no commercially satisfactory dwarfing understock for peaches such as is available for apples. The home gardener might want to experiment by grafting on to *Prunus tomentosa* but results to date have been variable.

PEAR UNDERSTOCK

Seedlings from the domestic pear, *Pyrus communis,* and Bartlett are recommended. As there is no dwarfing rootstock in pears comparable to those for apples, rootstock of certain Quince cultivars have been used. Unfortunately Quince understock have proven to be root tender to winter cold in all but the mildest parts of the country.

Where they can be grown they produce large fruit of superb quality. With some diligent searching, you can likely find rootstocks of the Quince Ungers (Quince A) Quince C and Provenance. Winter protection of the root system with 8 to 15 cm (3 to 6 in) of straw may help pears grafted onto dwarfing Quince understock in borderline areas.

PLUM UNDERSTOCK

Most commercially grown plums are grafted on Myrobalan *(Prunus cerasifera)*, producing a full-sized tree. The home gardener can achieve dwarf plums by using Western Sand cherry *(Prunus besseyi)* and Nanking cherry *(Prunus tomentosa)*, as rootstocks except with the Damson variety which is not compatible with these rootstocks. Using Western Sand and Nanking, the varieties Shiro, a yellow plum, and Grand Duke, a blue plum, have been reported to produce large fruit of superb quality, ten days earlier than on other rootstocks.

NECTARINE UNDERSTOCK

Nectarines, essentially a peach without fuzz, can be grafted on any understock suitable for peach.

LOCATING UNDERSTOCK

If you want to experiment with your own grafting, I suggest you contact the extension horticulturalist in your area for the names of nurseries where you could obtain these understocks. The information office of your provincial or state agriculture department will have the name, address and phone number of the extension horticulturalist nearest you .

How to Graft

Quite a few years ago, my father and I attempted to graft our MacIntosh apples to what we thought was a dwarf variety. I think it was a Malling type. Today, I'm having trouble explaining to my kids the meaning of the word "dwarf." Did we buy the wrong rootstock?

If you indeed bought a Malling variety, you should have had a dwarf or at least a semi-dwarf tree. The problem may have been with the actual graft procedure. Can you remember how far up the rootstock you did the graft?

I'd say about 20 cm (8 in) from the base at the initial planting.

And you replanted the tree in deeper soil leaving the graft exposed?

Yes. My father had told me the tree would need to be replanted but I didn't do it until a year or so later. I wasn't exactly sure how much of the trunk to bury but I figured the soil should come right up to the graft.

I suspect you covered up too much of the trunk. You have to take care at planting or in later years that the soil does not come in contact with the trunk above the graft. If roots are formed above the graft, the dwarfing effect of the rootstock will be lost and the graft will grow to a full-sized tree.

Grafting is quite simple, but exacting work. First you must realize that with woody plants like fruit trees, the only living parts of the tree are the leaves and a thin layer of tissue just under the bark called the cambium layer. This layer of plant cells conducts the water and nutrients from the roots to the leaves. The rest of the trunk and the branches, including the bark, is dead plant tissue. To execute a successful graft the live cambium tissue of a desirable fruiting variety must be brought in secure, vital contact with the cambium tissue of the trunk or branch of a compatible rootstock. Usually this means any apple variety can be grafted to another apple (even a crabapple) but apple cannot be grafted to a distant relative such as the oak. Nectarine (a fuzzless peach) can be grafted to peach, and pear can be grafted to its near relative, quince.

Our questioner was attempting a whip or tongue graft which is commonly used for fruit trees. With tongue grafting the rootstock is normally a rooted single stem, unbranched cutting or seedling. It should be 1 to 2 cm (1/4 to 1/2 in) in diameter at the point where you want to make the graft. Grafting on to the rootstock should not be attempted until the rootstock has been growing a full season in the location where the graft will be performed. The graft is normally made about 9 cm (3 in) above the ground. However, with dwarf apples on M9 rootstock you may help support the tree by grafting

30 cm (12 in) above grade. One or two years later the tree should be replanted deeper, burying 20 cm (8 in) of the trunk of the rootstock below grade. This buried portion of the trunk will eventually root out and act like the buried portion of a hydro pole to support the tree. Trees grafted in this way are sometimes available at nurseries.

Choose a branch in the dormant stage from the most recent year's growth on the fruit tree you wish to propagate. This branch, called a scion in grafting, should be as close as possible to the diameter of the rootstock. This will ensure maximum contact between the thin cambium layer of each stock, providing a quick and strong union. The scion should contain two or three buds with a smooth space clear of buds at the lower end. It need not be the growing tip of a branch and any excess length beyond three buds should be pruned off.

The cut in the top of the understock should be exactly the same angle as the cut made in the scion. Both must be smooth not wavy,

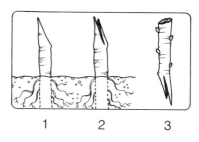

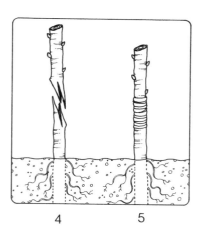

Tongue grafting
1. To prepare the rootstock, make a long, sloping cut 2.5 to 6.5 cm (1 to 2½ in) long at the top of the stock.
2. Make a second downward cut starting one-third the distance from the tip to the base of the first cut.
3. Prepare the scion by making two cuts at the base, the same length as the cuts on the stock.
4. Slip the stock and scion together, the tongues interlocking.
5. The graft is then tied and wrapped with electrical tape.

or a satisfactory union will not take place. This requires a very sharp knife so each cut can be made with one stroke to achieve uniformity and smoothness. On a 1 cm (1/3 in) diameter scion and understock, the surface of the cut should be 2.5 to 3 cm (3/4 to 1 in) long. Larger stock will result in proportionately larger surfaces.

A second cut is then made in both the understock and scion. Do this about one third of the way down from the tip and at a more acute angle than the first cut so that it follows the same line. Take care the grain of the wood is not split in the process. The objective is to dovetail the tongues and cuts in the scion and understock. I recommend you practise this operation on branches of similar size before you start on the understock. You need a smooth, tight fit with the cambium layer of the rootstock and the scion in contact along as much of the surfaces as possible. The lower tip of the scion should not overhang the rootstock as this may cause the formation of large callus knots in later years.

The graft is then secured with strong light butcher cord, #18 crochet cotton would be ideal. After the union is tied, it is covered with grafting wax to prevent dehydration which would abort the union. Another method of binding is to use black plastic electrical tape and wrap the graft like you would a hockey stick handle. This eliminates the string and the need of grafting wax. After growth begins and the graft has united, the binding must be carefully removed to prevent it from constricting subsequent growth.

It is feasible to graft a scion of smaller diameter to understock with a larger diameter. Do not, however, centre the scion on the understock. This would preclude the essential contact of the cambium layers of each. Rather, move the scion to one side of the understock to ensure that the live tissues contact over as much an area as possible.

Tongue grafting when the scion is considerably smaller than the rootstock The scion is placed on one side of the stock and the slanting cut is not made through the entire stock.

Budding

My question relates to a grafting problem. I have successfully helped a friend graft an apple tree but when I tried the same method on my peach tree it just didn't take.

Did you graft part of a branch or just the bud?

We used the middle section of a branch, sharpened the one end and inserted it into a cut on the new tree.

I believe you are describing tongue grafting. For stone fruits (plum, cherry and peach) budding may work better than grafting. With these trees, the wood often does not split well enough for grafting. But the bark can easily be manipulated for budding.

By budding you mean taking only the bud and a bit of bark and inserting it into the new tree?

Right. You may find that this works better.

For a successful bud graft, an actively growing shoot from the current year's growth should be chosen for budstock. The leaves should be mature and the shoot itself firm and woody with a bud at the axil where the leaves and shoot join. As with tongue grafting, the tip and the base of the current year's growth, now called the budwood, are discarded. A good piece of budwood will yield several buds. All the leaves on the budwood are pruned off leaving about 2 cm (1/2 in) of the leaf stem as a handle.

If more than a few minutes lapse between the trimming of the budwood and the insertion of the actual bud into the cut in the rootstock, then mist the budwood and store it out of the sun in a plastic bag to avoid any dehydrating.

Choose a smooth area on the stem of a compatible, well-established rootstock about 10 cm (4 in) from grade. Using a sharp knife, make a vertical cut through the bark about 3 cm (1 in) long. Then, using a rocking motion of the knife, make a horizontal cut about 2 cm (5/8 in) long at the top of the vertical cut. Before you remove the knife, give it a twist to raise the bark, opening a T-shaped incision.

Now use the knife to remove the bud from the budstick by cutting from below upward so that the entire thickness of the bark is removed at the point of the bud approximately 1 cm (1/3 in) deep. Continue up the stem with this cut to about 3 cm (1 in) beyond the bud. Slide the knife back out. At a point about 1 to 2 cm (1/3 to 2/3 in) above the bud, make a horizontal cut just through the bark, making sure you don't cut right through to the vertical cut. This shallow cut will leave some wood underneath the bud still attached to the budstick.

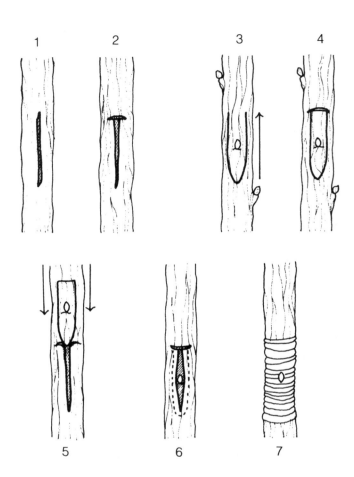

Budding
1. Make a vertical cut about 2.5 cm (1 in) long in the stock.
2. Make a horizontal cut through the bark about one-third the distance around the stock. Give the knife a slight twist to open the two flaps of bark.
3. To prepare the bud, slice a cut about 1.3 cm (½ in) below the bud and about 2.5 cm (1 in) beyond the bud.
4. About 2 cm (¾ in) above the bud make a horizontal cut through the bark and into the wood, permitting the removal of the bud piece.
5. Insert the shield into the stock by pushing it downward under the two flaps of bark.
6. The horizontal cuts on the shield and the stock should be even.
7. Tie the bud to the stock with electrical tape.

Taking the bud between the thumb and forefinger press it down firmly against the budstick and slide it sideways. A small core of wood comprising the sap conducting tissue must remain with the bud. If this small core of wood remains attached to the budstick, leaving a hole in the bud, there is no chance of success. The core of wood will make the vital contact with the living cambium tissue just below the bark of the rootstock. To accomplish this union the bud, now called a shield because of its shape, is pushed down into the open flap of the T incision in the bark of the rootstock until the upper cut of the shield is opposite the upper horizontal cut in the rootstock. This should be a snug fit, with the shield covered by the flaps of the T incision except for the bud itself.

Promptly, to avoid drying the tissue, wrap the incision area with black plastic electrical tape, leaving the bud exposed. Remove this tape in about a month's time to avoid constricting the growth. The bark will have begun to heal over by this time.

The bud will now be dormant until growth starts the next spring. In the spring, prune the rootstock about 1 cm (1/3 in) above the bud. Remove all the growth that comes from the rootstock other than the grafted bud. You have made yourself a new creation that should serve you well for years.

When to Graft and Bud

I tried to do a graft last year but the grafted branch just shrivelled up and died.

When did you do the graft?

In the summer. Late June, I think.

Had the buds on the branch begun to break open?

I don't really remember.

I strongly suspect that you left the graft too late. It is critical to the success of the grafting that the scion is dormant but that the rootstock has begun spring growth with the sap rising freely from the roots. If the leaf buds of the scion have begun to swell and break open, they will continue to do so even after the graft has been executed. At this point there is no union with the rootstock to draw moisture from the roots. The scion will lose its meagre moisture supply to the expanding leaves, and so wither and die. For this reason, the scion must be selected in late winter just before any growth begins. It can be stored in a plastic bag in the vegetable crisper of your refrigerator. This effectively retards the development of the scion until the rootstock has begun growth.

Budding (bud grafting) is done in the summer when the bark of the rootstock is loose enough to be carefully lifted from the cambium layer and the bud to be grafted is mature. Below are the approximate dates when this should be viable.

Pear   July 10 to July 20
Apple   July 15 to August 10
Plum   August 10 to September 1
Cherry (on Mazzard) July 20 to August 1
Cherry (on Mahaleb) August 15 to September 1
Peach, Apricot, Nectarine   August 20 to September 10

These dates are not set in stone. Some professional grafters bud graft all species in June. If the bark can be readily separated from the cambium layer beneath, then the bud graft may be done on any species in June.

Novelty Grafting

I ask this question more out of curiosity than anything else. When we take our weekly trip north starting in the spring, we pass a peculiar fruit tree that blossoms at different times on different parts of the tree. We have had countless discussions on the cause. Can you tell us what would make a tree react this way?

What you are probably seeing is a fruit tree that has had a number of different varieties grafted onto it. It certainly can provide an interesting sight and make quite a conversation piece.

People often have room for only one fruit tree but have difficult choosing which fruit variety to plant. If you like five different kind of apples, five-in-one grafting is the way to go. The simplest wa of achieving this result is to buy a five-in-one apple tree at a nursery. If, however, you want the satisfaction of choosing your own varietie and grafting them yourself, then the method is not complex.

Choose the most suitable understock, making sure you have a many well-placed branches as varieties (see page 54). Plant th young tree a year in advance of the grafting to allow it to becom established. The understock can be one of the varieties you wan in the final tree but not necessarily; you can graft all the varietie in.

One piece of dormant scion wood of the previous year's growt of each variety is necessary for the graft. The diameter of that woo should be as close as possible to the diameter of the branches o the understock. The procedure and timing is exactly the same a

70

whip or tongue grafting (see pp. 64 to 66). except you make the graft 8 to 32 cm (3 to 12 in) from the base of each branch rather than right on the trunk. Otherwise follow the same procedure, grafting each variety onto a different branch. All other branches on the rootstock not used in grafting should be removed at the time of grafting or one month later after the grafts have "taken." This forces all the growth into the new branches. All varieties should begin bearing within one to two years if grafted on a dwarf understock.

Chapter 4: Fruit Bushes

Black Currants Drop

I have six black currant bushes which I planted five or six years ago. They are nice healthy bushes, the leaves are green and there is new growth each year. Each spring they flower well and form little green berries and each year all the berries and flowers fall off overnight. I have not picked a single berry off them yet.

The problem is a fairly common one with certain varieties of black currant. What you saw forming under the flower was the ovary. To develop into a berry the flower must be pollinated — pollen from the anthers must be placed on the stigma of the flower.

In general, black currants are self-fruitful; there is no need to have different varieties to achieve cross-pollination. However, there are several varieties which trace their ancestry to a variety called Boskoop Giant, which have a peculiar flower structure. The form of the flower is such that it cannot self-pollinate and prevents bees from getting into the flower to do the job. If no pollination takes place, the flower and ovary drop as yours did.

Is there anything I can do about it?

I am afraid the only answer is to change varieties. The varieties Topsy and Baldwin are excellent producers of top quality fruit. Consort is not quite as good but does have resistance to currant rust — a disease of black currants. Magnus is another good variety.

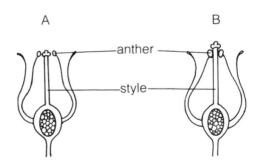

Black currants drop
Where the style in the flowers in any given cluster is close to the position shown in (A), pollination and fruit development occur. In position (B), the flower and ovary will likely abort because the style is above the anther.

The original research into the cause of black currants aborting was done in England. By carefully examining the flowers of many varieties, scientists discovered a notable difference in the length of the style in varieties descended from Boskoop Giant (see illustration).

Unfortunately, because the poor cropping varieties produce lots of new growth for propagating cuttings, some nurseries, in ignorance, prefer to produce them.

Blueberries: Selecting Varieties

We live in North Bay and would like to grow blueberries. Is there any special variety that is more suited to the climate up here?

For colder areas you can try Northland or Rancocas. Northland is a hybrid of the cultivated highbush blueberry and the lowbush blueberry which is found in the wild. The plants are fairly short and in winter snow cover will provide considerable protection. Rancocas is fairly hardy and has medium-small berries with a fairly good flavour. Both these varieties ripen earlier than other varieties. Early ripening is desirable in areas with a short growing season.*

So can I just choose one of these and plant it?

Choose more than one variety. Larger fruit and better fruit set occurs when cross-pollination by honeybees or wild bumblebees takes place.

Great improvements have been made in blueberry varieties. In addition to Northland and Rancocas the following varieties of highbush blueberries have produced good-quality fruit:
Berkeley: A very vigorous, open, spreading, and very productive bush. Fruit clusters are large and medium loose. The Berkeley berries are largest of all — light blue, medium firm, crisp and with a mild-sweet flavour.
Bluecrop: An upright and vigorous bush with a tendency to overbear. Young bushes are slightly vulnerable to cold winters. Fruit clusters are large and medium loose. The berries are large, very light blue, firm and subacid (bland in flavour).
Blueray: A vigorous, upright and hardy bush. Fruit clusters are large and rather tight. Berries are large, light blue, firm, subacid and aromatic.

---

*Free copies of "Plant Hardiness Zones in Canada" available from:
Information Division, Agriculture Canada, Ottawa, K1A 0C7. Cat. No. A52-3873.
In the United States copies @ 25¢ each of "Plant Hardiness Zone Map" Misc.
Pub. No. 814, available from:
Superintendent of Documents, U.S. Government Printing Office, Washington, D.C.
20402.

Highbush blueberries *(Vaccimium corymbosum)* are generally hardy in milder regions (zones 6a, 6b and 7a). Snow, however, makes an excellent protective cover. Enclosing the blueberry patch with a snow fence to encourage deep drifting may be sufficient to protect bushes in borderline zones where snow is prevalent.

The lowbush blueberry *(Vaccimium augustifolium)*is found growing naturally from Newfoundland to Manitoba and is hardier in the winter cold. It is an extremely important commercial export crop in Nova Scotia and New Brunswick. Most connoisseurs consider the lowbush blueberry superior in flavour to its taller, highbush cousin.

Blueberries: pH Requirements

On a visit to a local nursery I noticed they had blueberry bushes for sale. My mouth began to water just at the thought of being able to pick fresh blueberries from my garden. I bought some and planted them. They didn't grow, the leaves turned yellow and despite my best efforts, they just faded away. What went wrong?

The most likely cause was the pH level of the soil. Blueberries require an acid soil. Nor are they tolerant of heavy clay soils or poorly drained soils. Midsummer heat combined with draught will also affect them adversely.

It sounds like I had better give up on blueberries.

Not at all! What it means is that conditions conducive to successful blueberries seldom occur naturally. You have to cause them. But then, that's the challenge and excitement of growing something different. To take good pictures with a 35 mm camera you must study aperture, film speed, shutter speed and composition or you will ruin a lot of film. To grow blueberries, you must know about soil pH, drainage, hardiness zones and a few other interesting facts. This information is all available. You just need to study and apply it.

Blueberries are long-lived bushes so proper soil preparation is a sound investment that will return flavourful fruit for many years.

A sandy or sandy loam soil which drains well is best. However, the home gardener can construct a soil that will work even in heavy clay areas.

First you must determine the pH of the existing soil and the area of your garden that will drain well even when frozen. It should receive at least a half day's sun. Sun all day long is best. A soil can be acidified within certain limits. The pH level is scaled between 0 and 14 — 7.0 is neutral, above 7.0 is alkaline, below 7.0 is acid. However to understand the task of acidifying, realize that pH values are logarithmic. This means that soil with a pH of 5.0 is ten times as acid as a soil of 6.0 and soil with a pH of 4.0 is 100 times as acid as soil with a 6.0 pH reading.

The optimum pH level for blueberries appears to be 4.3 to 4.8. Experience has shown that the upper limits of pH that can be acidified to suit blueberries is a value of 6.7 and even soil with a value of 6.5 is difficult to modify. So you must begin by having your soil tested (see Chapter 1), which will give nutrient levels plus pH reading.

Before establishing your blueberry bed, you will need frequent readouts on pH. You should consider buying pH paper strips which indicate pH over various ranges. These are available at some garden centres, scientific supply houses* and stores specializing in hydroponic gardening. Some garden centres have pH metres and can test your soil for you.

It is virtually impossible to obtain and maintain a pH of 4.5 in a small island of soil surrounded by a sea of soil that is 100 times more alkaline. For this reason, you are wise not to attempt to scatter blueberry bushes in various solo locations throughout the garden. For the same reason a long, narrow acidified strip is impractical.

The best shape of plot then for your blueberries is square or oblong. Allow 1.2 m × 1.2 m (4 ft x 4 ft) for each plant. A plot 3.7 m × 4.9 m (12 ft × 16 ft) would contain twelve plants. At maturity, these should readily produce 4.5 L (4 quarts) per plant per year.

To obtain excellent drainage, to help isolate the soil from the neutralizing effect of surrounding, less acid soil and to incorporate organic content, the preferred method is to construct a raised bed. From the yield figures given above, you can calculate the number of plants you may need and then work out the plot size. If your native soil is sandy or sandy loam, then this should be modified with fibrous acid peat moss. Check the acidity of the peat before you buy. Hopefully, you can find peat moss with pH values of 4.5 or less. This both supplies the necessary organic matter and acidifies the soil. Add 15 to 20 cm (6 to 8 in) of peat to the entire area and mix thoroughly with the top 10 to 15 cm (6 to 8 in) of soil. Try to add a further 10 cm (4 in) of two-thirds peat and one-third sandy loam to raise the plot to 30 cm (12 in) above the surrounding grade.

The above is the preferred method of lowering pH. However, with sandy or sandy loam soil, pH can be lowered by using sulphur. Add sulphur at the rate of 330 to 660 g per 9 m² (3/4 to 1 1/2 lb per 100 ft²) for each full point the soil registers above pH 4.5. The lower rate is for sandy soils and the higher for sandy loams. For example, a sandy loam with a pH 5.5 would require 660 g per 9 m² (1 1/2 lb per 100 ft²) to lower the pH one full point to 4.5. This sulphur should be applied the year before planting and be thoroughly mixed into the top 15 to 20 cm (6 to 8 in) of soil.

---

*BDH Chemicals, 350 Evans Avenue, Toronto, Ontario M8Z 1K5.

However, do not assume because you have applied the recommended amount of sulphur or peat moss that the pH is correct. Soils vary enormously in their response to acidifying techniques. It may take double the amount of sulphur recommended or a combination of peat moss and sulphur to achieve the correct pH. Before it is effective, the sulphur must be oxidized by soil bacteria and this takes up to three months. You can monitor the change using pH papers after two to three months. If no further change has taken place, this will determine if more sulphur and/or peat moss is required to bring the pH to 4.5.

With heavy clay soils the only practical route is to buy sandy topsoil and mix it with acidic peat moss at the ratio of one-third soil and two-thirds peat moss. A 30 cm (12 in) raised bed will be required. This can be retained by sloping the sides and sodding or by a curb of timbers, blocks or vertically installed sidewalk slabs. The clay soil underneath the bed should be dug as deeply as possible to ensure drainage before the amended soil is applied.

Transplanting Elderberries

I have access to lots of elderberry bushes which I pick to make great wine and jam. They are about a mile away from my home where I have a good moist site for them. When would be the best time to move them closer to home?

The moist site is ideal. Any deciduous (leaf dropping) shrub or tree is best moved just as the leaves begin to fall in the autumn or early in the spring before the leaf buds break. Because you are dealing with wet locations, I would favour fall moving. However, if we have a lot of fall rain, then spring moving will work equally well.

Do I have to prune them down a bit first?

Yes. The principle here is that moving a plant from a site where it has been growing for a number of years is bound to cause the loss of some of the root system. The top growth should be pruned off in proportion to the lost roots — usually about half of the growth. However, the elder does propagate from suckers arising from the roots. It may be quite feasible to simply lift out individual suckers growing around the bushes with a spade. These would then be pruned back by half. If you elect to lift a whole bush, I would consider using a bushel basket to carry it in. You could dig a hole the size of the bushel and plant the elder, bushel and all, at the same depth it was in its former site. If part of the bushel sticks up above the grade, don't be concerned. The bottom will soon rot and you can lift the top off and discard it.

Moving fruit bushes is often a desirable thing to do. If you are planning to move and are aware of the impending move far enough in advance, root pruning a year ahead of time will ensure a successful operation. Simply take a spade and cut the root system by driving the spade the full depth into the ground in a circle around the shrub. The diameter of the circle should be slightly smaller than the eventual root ball you will move — in this case, slightly smaller than a bushel.

You do not cut the roots going vertically down from the bush but by cutting the horizontal ones, you encourage branching of the roots and the growth of many fine new roots which will support the shrub in its new location.

With deciduous shrubs like elder, it is not essential that all the soil in the root ball come with the shrub if it is moved in the dormant stage. However, the more soil that is moved, leaving the root system intact, the quicker new growth will form and the less top pruning you will have to do.

Growing Grapes

I want to grow grapes, but the spot I've chosen is right next to the house, so that I can build a trellis. How much sun do grapes need?

Grapes need a well-drained site that receives a minimum of half a day's sun. Full sun is better. Trellises are often built next to the house, which may cast a shadow, so this is an important consideration.

How do I know when the grapes are ready to be picked?

Grapes are not really mature until they have reached their maximum sugar content. Once the fruit has been harvested, there is no appreciable increase in sugar content. Unlike most kinds of fruit, grapes do not continue to "ripen" after picking. So even well-coloured grapes should not be cut until they are sweet. Tasting them is the best maturity test.

Each grape vine will occupy a space of about 1.2 m (4 ft) wide on a trellis and 2.4 m (8 ft) wide on wires. Bear in mind that grapes should bear for twenty years or more, so build the trellis to last. If a wire trellis is to be used with the grapes planted in a row, then you will need 2.4 m (8 ft) posts, 10 cm (4 in) in diameter of cedar, locust or white oak. Do not creosote; it is toxic. Copper naphanate wood preservative applied to the portion of the post in the ground is an excellent investment, as the posts can be carrying a lot of weight. They can be further strengthened by backfilling the hole with dry, premixed concrete. Soil moisture will turn it into concrete.

Set the posts at 4.8 m (16 ft) intervals. Intermediary posts can be 7 cm (3 in) in diameter. The posts should be set with 1.5 m (5 ft) above grade and 90 cm (3 ft) below. Three 10-gauge galvanized wires are strung taut between the poles, one 60 cm (24 in) above the grade, one 105 cm (3 1/2 ft) and one at the top of the posts.

The soil line on the dormant vine will show you the depth it was in the nursery. Plant it about 5 cm (2 in) deeper in the prepared soil. Plant container-grown plants the same depth that they are in the container.

Many varieties of grapes, especially some of the French hybrids, tend to overbear and benefit from bunch thinning. All bunches should be removed for the first two years to promote vine growth. Vines that have reached the top wire the third year should be allowed to bear a light crop of one bunch on each of the stronger shoots. Overloaded vines will produce fruit of poor quality, with small straggly bunches. It is important to remove the bunches before the blossoms open, usually before the middle of June. At this time the bunches are easily pinched off. Leave one bunch per shoot, with two on a few of the stronger ones. In some cases it is advisable to remove all bunches from the weaker secondary shoots.

If thinning is left until after the fruit is set, many of the benefits will be lost. The remaining bunches will not increase in size to the same extent, and will not make up for those removed. However, it may still be necessary to thin to save the vine from winter injury. If the actual vine of the grape plant has to compete with the fruit for plant food, it cannot store enough food to give it the vigour necessary to with stand the rigors of winter.

Pruning Grapes

I have some grape vines growing on wire supports. There is lots of growth but a very poor crop of small, straggly bunches.

The problem probably lies in lack of proper pruning and thinning of bunches. Grapes absolutely need correct pruning to crop at anywhere near their potential.

Home gardeners often have such an emotional attachment to their plants that they find it painful to even contemplate pruning, let alone do it. Many plants, however, simply will not be productive without knowledgeable pruning. Grapes are a prime example of this.

INITIAL PRUNING

The process begins when you purchase your vines. These can be bought from nurseries early in the spring, either bare root and dormant or growing in containers. Many nurseries do not prune the vines ready for planting. The first operation is to prune off all but the strongest cane. Further prune back that cane to two plainly visible branch buds. This will appear harsh but is necessary to ensure that first flush of vigorous growth.

PRUNING AND TRAINING THE YOUNG VINE

With the pruning at planting you have two buds left that should produce canes. If, as growth begins, more than two appear, prune off the weakest ones. Stake and tie the remaining two upright and tie the stake to the bottom wire. The strongest of these two canes should reach the bottom wire and possibly the middle wire the first year. The weakest may be pruned off early the first summer but at the latest must be removed with the early spring pruning the following year.

The remaining cane should continue to grow upward the second summer. When it reaches the second and third wires, it should be drawn taut vertically and tied with twine to these wires.

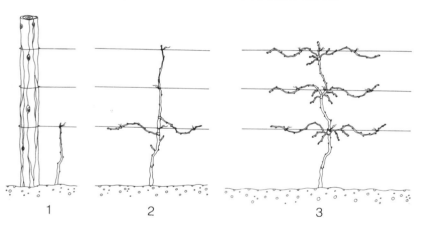

1   2   3

Pruning grapes
1. After one year's growth the vine is attached to the bottom wire. The weaker secondary cane left at time of planting has been removed.
2. After two years of growth, the tip above the top wire has been removed. Selected lateral canes have been tied to the lower wire and pruned back to five buds.
3. A mature vine. All canes have been removed except one on each wire in each direction. These form the fruiting canes. They are cut back in accordance to the vigour of the previous cane production (see Table). Spurs are left for cane renewal.

In March or early April, this leader cane should be pruned back to the height of the top wire to encourage branching. Meanwhile the vine will have sent out lateral canes beginning near the grade. Prune off all lateral canes except the strongest to be trained one along the bottom wire in each direction. At the same time, prune back these laterals to five buds on each.

At pruning time the third spring, you should be able to select a strong lateral to go each direction on each wire. Prune these back to five buds each, and tie them securely to the wires. Prune off all other canes. This selection can also be done during the third growing season if growth has not been sufficient during the second summer.

SUBSEQUENT ANNUAL BALANCED PRUNING

The grape bears fruit only on the previous summer's growth. Letting the vine go unpruned, accumulating excessive old growth, will greatly reduce the yield and produce poor fruit. Balanced pruning takes into account the amount of growth produced by the vine during the previous growing season (indicating its health and vigour) in determining how much fruit the vine should bear in the current year. Accordingly, the first step in pruning is to remove all excess wood except for six canes from the growth produced during the previous season, and three or four short canes (containing 2 to 3 buds each) which are called renewal spurs and will produce canes and fruit for the following year. The canes which are left should be chocolate brown in colour, slightly thicker than a pencil, and should grow as close as possible to the main trunk. Then, using a small spring balance, such as a fish scale with a string or metal scoop attached, weigh the prunings you have just removed. The weight of those prunings will tell how much to shorten the remaining long canes. according to the following table:

	Weight of one-year prunings		Number of buds to leave for fruiting	
	pounds	kilos		
Less than	1	.5	Less than	30
	1	.5		30
	2	.9		40
	3	1.4		50
	4	1.8		60
	5	2.3		70
	5	2.3		70
	6	2.7		80
More than	6	2.7		80 plus

For example, a vine from which you have removed 2 pounds of pruning should be allowed only 40 buds on its remaining canes, or 7 buds per cane. The canes should then be pruned back further to the correct number of buds (Fig. 3).

Although the balanced pruning method is by far the best method for pruning grapes, some home owners may not have the time or interest to use this method. In this case, the six canes which remain after all excess growth should simply be shortened so that they each contain about eight buds. Again the three or four renewal spurs must be left.

WINTER PROTECTION

Where temperatures fall below -28°C (-20°F), or where winter injury of the vines is experienced, winter protection should be provided. The fan system of training makes this protection possible. The trunk is kept below the bottom wire, and the arms are trained to the wires as shown. Each fall, loosen the vines from the wires and bend them, without breaking them, to the ground. Lay the vines flat under the

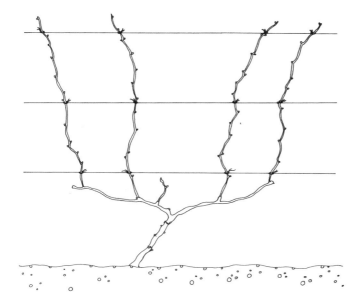

Wintering grape vines
1. The fan system of training, shown immediately after pruning, is preferred where winter protection is required.

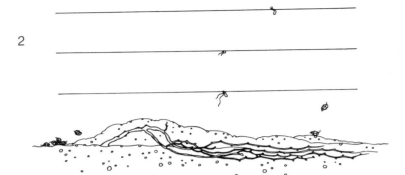

2. In the fall the vines are loosened from the wires and bent down to the ground. Cover the vines with about 3 in (9 cm) of soil.

wire, and cover them with soil to a depth of 8 to 10 cm (3 to 4 in) In the spring the vines are uncovered, three to five canes are se lected from the previous season's growth and tied to the wires leaving thirty to sixty buds, depending on the vigour of the vine. An other canes should be pruned off. Every few years, as the arm become thick and hard to bend, it will be necessary to renew ther by selecting a cane originating from or near the head of the trunk and establishing new arms from which to select the canes.

RENOVATING OLD VINES

Grape vines which have been neglected for many years requir severe pruning in order to begin producing quality fruit again. Cu the plants back severely at the normal pruning time, removing a much of the older wood as possible. Follow the same basic prunin design as for regular pruning. Any old wood which cannot be re moved with one pruning may be cut off with the regular pruning th following season.

Pruning Raspberries

How do you prune raspberries and when?

Are these the regular red raspberries that bear one crop of fruit in July?

Yes, but my crop was not very good this year and I suspect I am not pruning correctly. I am going to have to do something. There are new canes coming up from the roots and the row is getting wider and wider.

Yes, you will have to control the width of the row by pruning off any cane that makes the row wider than 45 cm (18 in). If you allow the rows to get wider than this, it makes picking difficult and does not increase the yield. Pruning can be done by hand with pruning sheers. You should regard a raspberry sucker coming from the roots early in the spring and summer beyond the 45 cm (18 in) width as a raspberry weed. They can be hoed off or rototilled under a lot easier when they are young than by hand pruning when they are older. A herbicide containing paraquat diquat applied to the emerging suckers would also destroy them.

I have just gleaned my last few raspberries. Is there anything I can do now?

This is the time to do the major pruning and thinning. The regular red raspberry has perennial roots but biennial canes. These come up mainly from the roots one year; bear fruit and then die the second year. All the canes that have borne fruit should be pruned off at ground level along with the weak new growth.

Some of the new growth is very tall, 150 cm (60 in) or more. They are going to be difficult to pick next year and may fall over.

Quite true, but I don't recommend that you top them off to the 120 cm (48 in) level until late March or early April. Topping them now will encourage soft new growth that will be vulnerable to winter kill.

Caution: Paraquat diquat is a toxic material. Care should be taken during application to avoid skin contact. Read all labels and wear rubber gloves.

Pruning raspberries in the hot weather of late July and early August is the job that has pushed the price of commercially produced raspberries up and out of sight. Growers just can't find workers who are willing to perform this hot, arduous task in the proper way. As a result, fewer and fewer raspberries are grown commercially. However, it also means the rewards for growing your own are a high dollar return as well as a fruit flavour that knows no equal.

To get the maximum yield from raspberries, the best procedure is summer pruning. It has the additional benefit of minimizing disease which can be rampant on the dying canes that have borne fruit.

Do not completely thin out the new growth until March or April. Otherwise you could encourage the late growth of remaining shoots which would be susceptible to winter injury. The objective at the final spring pruning is a 45 cm (18 in) row with at least 15 cm (6 in) between all canes.

There are also a number of "mosaic" virus diseases that attack raspberries, which should be pruned out when recognized. The name refers to the effect they have on the appearance of the leaves. Pale green to yellow blotches develop on the surface of the leaves. This mottling can be fine or coarse; confined to the lower leaves or present throughout the plant. Frequently puckering takes place and the leaves can be narrower than normal. The most pronounced symptoms occur during the rapid growth in June. Growth is stunted and there will be little new growth on infected canes. The fruit will be small, sparse, and more crumbly than healthy plants. The other most common virus-induced symptom is leaf curl — a pronounced rippling and curling under of the new leaves as they appear.

If you are setting out new rows of raspberries, the best preventative control is to buy certified raspberry canes. The provincial governments supply a nucleus of disease-free stock to co-operating nurseries, who in turn multiply the stock under controlled conditions and make it available to growers. Your nearest horticultural research station (either federal or provincial) or provincial horticultural extension agent can put you in touch with these nurseries. Some of these are retailers, the others can give you names of retail nurseries who sell their certified stock. I recommend you plant only certified stock. It is well worth any problems you might have locating it.

Viruses and other diseases are contagious and difficult to eradicate once they are in the garden. Plants never recover from them and spreading to other plants is certain. Pruning out suspected plants can slow down the spread of disease. Systematically and thoroughly destroying all wild raspberries within 150 m (500 ft) is an essential part of prevention and control.

Alternative to Pruning Raspberries

Pruning raspberries is such a boring, ongoing process. Is there anything I could do to stop them from spreading in the first place?

Yes. Dig a 30 cm (12 in) narrow trench and install a sheet of .06 mm thick black plastic vertically from the surface to the bottom of the trench. Then fill in the trench. Building supply stores sell this for placing under poured concrete footings to prevent rapid dehydration of the concrete.

Could I use green garbage bags?

I find that they do not work as well. Polyethylene sheeting breaks down fairly rapidly when exposed to sunlight. Where the plastic is near the surface of the soil, the sun would penetrate the green plastic garbage bag and cause breakdown. You also need the physical strength of 6 mil (1/4 in) thick sheeting to prevent accidental penetration by garden tools. Garbage bags are only about 2 mil thick.

Planting Strawberries

I want to set out a strawberry planting. How should I space the plants?

Traditionally, strawberries have been planted in rows about 1.2 m (48 in) apart and about 60 cm (24 in) apart in the rows early in the spring. Under proper conditions the plants root out and begin to send out runners, which are long stems with a plant forming at the end. By late summer with proper care a matted row solid with plants a metre wide could be formed. Only in the last few years have growers realized that this method resulted in overcrowding and poor production. The latest techniques involve a narrower row spacing — 80 cm to 1 m wide (32 to 39 in)— with the plants placed 60 to 75 cm (24 to 30 in) apart in the row. Runners that form are moved by hand, if necessary, to confine them to a row 30 cm (12 in) wide. Up to five plants or runners are allowed to form per 30 cm (12 in) of row. When this population is reached all subsequent runners are cut off.

How do you make those initial runners stay put?

A hair pin is an ideal way. A small stone will also work. Anything that holds the plantlet firmly to the ground so that it can root out.

A further refinement in this narrow row technique is to plant the row on raised ridge beds. Strawberries are prone to root rot. These diseases flourish in wet soil conditions. While root rot may not kill the plants it can reduce their vigour and lower production as much as 25 per cent. The raised beds drain more quickly, providing less opportunity for root rot organisms to flourish. The result is a higher yield of better quality strawberries.

However, because the raised beds dry out more quickly than flat ground, regular watering is essential. Do not attempt raised beds unless you have the water available as the fruit forms and matures.

If you plant as I suggested, 60 cm (24 in) apart in the row, no more than ten plants should be allowed to root in the space allotted between plants. These should all be formed by mid-August from an early spring planting.

Planting Strawberries: Timing

Can I plant next year's strawberry crop this fall? It seems to be so much harder to know when exactly to plant in the spring.

I would not plant strawberries in the fall. The best time is early spring as soon as the ground can be prepared. The plants should still be dormant. Normally the plants are either dug up in the fall by the nursery and stored dry at -2°C (29°F) or spring dug before they begin to grow. This is important. If the plant starts to grow, the limited supply of food stored in the leaves is expended putting out new roots. These roots will likely be lost in digging and replanting, leaving the plant in a weaker state.

Some retail nurseries, realizing that many gardeners do not really get into gear until the weather warms up, plant their strawberries in containers. These can then be moved to your garden any time in the spring.

Proper depth of planting is important if you are planting dormant bareroot plants. Too shallow or too deep cripples the new plant.

Strawberries runner the most prolifically in the spring and early summer, another good reason for an early start. The buds which determine next year's flowers and subsequent fruit are formed in August and early September. The runners should be out and rooted in by late August. Any runners formed after this will not crop well.

As with asparagus (Chapter 2), perennial weeds and grasses are the mortal enemy of strawberries. If you can keep your strawberry bed free of weeds you can recrop two or three or more times.

Renovation of the ridge rows will pose a problem if you have a narrow lawn mower which cannot be set high enough to miss the heart of the plant. A hedge clipper will also do the job nicely. Other than this modification, the following section on renovation applies. The second year, however, unless you feel the plant count was inadequate, all new runners must be removed. The same plant count per metre is maintained and the row is not allowed to widen whether it is on ridge beds or on the flat. In addition to improved production, the narrow rows minimize fungus disease, improve the possibilities of pollination and certainly make picking much easier.

Everbearing strawberries do best on this narrow ridge system. The procedure is the same as for June-bearing varieties except that because they do not have runners as prolifically, they must be planted closer together in the row — 20 to 30 cm (8 to 12 in) is the best spacing under good soil conditions. After an early spring planting fruit blossoms should be removed until mid-July to put all the growth potential into establishing the plant. From then on, they can be allowed to mature, and will produce a crop the first year of planting.

Everbearing strawberries will crop in June and July with some during the rest of the summer, but the main crop is stretched out through the fall. This means close attention must be paid to watering and insect control (particularly tarnished plant bugs) all summer. Production dwindles badly on plants over two years old. If there are sufficient new runners formed these can be pinned down and the two year plants removed.

Renovating Strawberries

I am not happy with my crop of strawberries. The plants look beautiful, but the leaves stand 20 to 25 cm (8 to 10 in) tall and you can't find a space between them.

How wide is the row?

We planted a single row with 30 cm (12 in) between the plants last spring. They grew well, putting out enough runners to make a dense mat about 1 m (39 in) wide. I was so pleased that the plants seemed so healthy. But the only place I got any real crop was along the edges of the row. In the centre there were hardly any berries.

The fact that your strawberries cropped well only along the edges of the row indicates overcrowding. In good soil, most strawberry varieties will produce too many runners. If the plantlets are allowed to root in, in a random fashion, they are usually too many plants for the available light. This is the main reason that the plants on the outside of the row where there is lots of light cropped better than those on the inside where the leaves formed a solid screen against the light.

What can I do about this now? The bed is already established.

You have to ruthlessly and systematically reduce the plant count per square metre of row. Now that the harvest has just finished, set your rotary mower about 3 cm (1 in) higher than you would cut your lawn, and mow off all the leaves. The next ruthless part is to run a rototiller which cuts a 30 cm (12 in) swath right down the centre of the row. In the two rows that remain, systematically, using a long ruler, allow a maximum of five plants per 30 cm (12 in) of row. Remove all the weaker plants to get the plant count down. Cut off and discard any new runners that form.

There is a sound scientific basis to the above recommendations. Any extra strawberry plants per square metre are strawberry weeds. They reduce the light essential to set and mature fruit. Managing runner activity and plant count per square metre is sound strawberry husbandry and gives the potential maximum yield.

Renovation of an existing strawberry patch should begin immediately after the last berries are picked. The main function of the cutting back with a lawn mower is to stimulate new growth. Strawberries normally go dormant after fruit bearing. Fruit buds for next year's crop are set in August and September on new growth. Pruning off all the leaves reverses the dormancy and initiates new growth in the old plants in preparation for bud set. Using this method, no new runners are necessary unless the plant count is below optimum.

Most strawberry varieties (except everbearing) put out an excessive number of runners resulting in too dense a population of plants. These have to compete for light, water, nutrients and air. Densely grown plants are more prone to fungus disease and incomplete pollination. If the centre of the row produces markedly less fruit than the sides or if the berry size drops off dramatically after the first planting, look to excessive plant count in the row.

Using a rototiller to remove a 30 cm (12 in) swath is based on the fact that the row in question was one metre wide. If the rototiller available to you is wider than 30 cm (12 in) the width tilled can be reduced by removing tynes. This will leave two rows about 30 cm (12 in) wide. Using a metre stick, the plant count in these rows should be reduced to no more than sixteen plants per metre by removing the weaker plants. If a tiller is not available, the row can be left 1 metre (thirty-two in) wide and the plant count per square metre (39 in × 39 in) reduced to about thirty-two. Any existing two year old rows I have checked have at least double this plant count per square metre (39 in × 39 in) to the detriment of fruit size and yield.

Counting plants per square metre can be confusing but a simple grid made of light lath will take the guesswork out of the job.

Renovation is also an excellent time to fertilize using a 10-15-20 or similar analysis granular fertilizer at the rate of 1.4 kilograms per 9 m² (3 lb per 100 ft²). Apply before the plants are mowed.

If you can keep out perennial grasses such as twitch grass (see Chapter 6) you can successfully renovate a strawberry patch each year for three or four years. New runners will form the following spring after renovation and these must be removed. Certainly a rototiller is the fastest and most efficient means of both cultivating and reducing the row to the previous year's width. Allowing the row to become wider than one metre will make picking very difficult.

Mowing time is an excellent opportunity to apply compost to the row. What you are doing with this type of culture is harvesting the same plants repeatedly. The plants tend to develop stems much like African Violets as they get older. Compost or a mixture of compost and soil or peat moss and soil thrown in around the plants to a depth of 2 cm (1/2 in) will provide fertile ground for the plants to root out from the stems for stronger subsequent growth.

Mulching Strawberries

Is it still considered a good idea to put straw on strawberry plants over the winter?

Yes. With the exception of the milder climatic area of southwestern B.C. strawberries benefit from the protection afforded by a 5 cm (2 in) layer of wheat, oat or rye straw. It protects the buds from winter injury. The straw, if applied at the proper time, prevents freezing and thawing of the soil which can actually heave the plants up, breaking the roots.

What is the proper time to apply the straw?

The plants must be fully dormant. If applied prematurely severe damage can be caused to the leaves and crown. Light frosts do not harm the plants but after the first hard frost where the temperature drops to -8°C (18°F) the straw should be applied loosely and evenly so that after it settles it is 5 cm (2 in) deep.

And when should it be taken off in the spring?

Monitor the early growth in the spring, and when the new leaves begin to grow and the foliage appears light yellow, remove one-half to two-thirds of the covering to the space between the rows. It acts as a weed preventer between the rows. The plants grow up through the straw left on the row. The fruit is held up off the soil by the straw, keeping it clean. When picking time rolls around, the straw provides a clean, soft place to kneel. Later it can be rototilled into the ground to provide essential organic matter.

Malformed Strawberries

My problem with strawberries is misshapen fruit. The fruit is rough looking and malformed and not as large as it should be.

What is the size of the fruit relative to the average size of properly shaped fruit?

I would say about two-thirds the size, but quite nubbly in appearance.

The cause of this is improper pollination of the strawberry flower. As you know, there are dozens of seeds on the outer surface of the strawberry fruit. The flesh of the strawberry only develops when the female parts of the flower (pistils) have been thoroughly impregnated with pollen by wind or insects. Professional strawberry growers put hives of honeybees near their strawberry fields to ensure proper pollination. The other cause of misshapen fruit is a frost when the flowers are open. Often it is just severe enough to injure some of the female parts of the blossom, making pollination and seed set impossible. The flesh in this area does not develop, giving the gnarled appearance to the fruit.

Frost at the time of full blossoming of strawberries is not unusual. The blossoms of a strawberry freeze at or below -1°C (30°F). Covering plants with newspaper if frost is predicted would likely provide protection. A continuous application of a fine mist of water when the temperature drops to -1°C (30°F) at the plant level will allow ice to form but prevent the temperature from dropping to critical levels.

The narrow ridge row technique (page 87) allows blossoms to be exposed to the prevailing winds and facilitates pollination. Certainly a hive of honeybees in the backyard will do the job admirably.

There is also a problem of misshapen fruit which is characterized by the fruit reaching only one quarter its normal size. There is a tight cluster of seeds on the end of the fruit opposite to the stem. While the fruit described earlier is usable, the fruit in this case is completely aborted. The cause here is injury to the forming seed by a .06 mm (1/4 in) coppery brown bug called the tarnished plant bug. This insect sucks on the seeds and destroys them. With the seed contents destroyed the flesh of the berry does not develop and aborted fruit results. The insect is controlled by spraying with Cygon 2E just as the first blossoms open and again ten days later. Spray in the late evening to avoid killing the bees.

Chapter 5: Bugs and Animals

Aphids

I have had a continuing battle with aphids on my broadbeans. Now they are on my tomatoes. What insecticides are recommended to control them on vegetables?

Usually aphids are fairly easy to control. The safest insecticides to use are rotenone or pyrethrum dusts.

Are they not poisonous, then?

Rotenone is probably the safest insecticide available because it is derived from plants. Pyrethrum is derived from the dried heads of several species of chrysanthemums, and in sunlight, it rapidly decomposes into non-poisonous compounds. Both are contact insecticides only. They have no residual action and must be applied directly to the aphid. If these do not bring quick control, I would try diazinon, dimethoate, endosulfan or malathion.

The name aphid covers a broad family of similar insects that can vary in appearance. The incredible thing about them is that if you plant cabbage, at some point the grey, waxy cabbage aphid will almost certainly appear out of nowhere. Plant beans, and the blue-black plant louse also found in the wild on burdocks will often take up residence. They even vary in colour to match the host plant. If they become too crowded they can develop wings to fly in search of new territory. Some species develop wings in response to cooler weather. As winter approaches, sexual forms appear which lay the overwintering eggs. The aphid is a truly resourceful bug.

They are sucking insects that can turn leaves yellow and malformed. A large population can cause the death of the leaf and host plant. If chemical control becomes necessary, usually one or two applications a week apart is effective. Be careful to observe the elapsed time required between the last application and harvest. Instructions will be printed on the label of the product you are using.

Soil Insect Control

Our problem is that we have cutworms really badly. We have had the garden for two years now and it is supposed to be a market garden that we are going to make money out of. Every time we plant we lose everything. We wanted to grow organically so we tried all the suggestions such as using wood ashes but the worms are just as bad this year as last. Everything just disappears.

The only non-chemical control of cutworms which works on transplants only is an open-ended tin can placed around the transplant at time of planting. A collar of tar paper about 8 cm (3 in) in diameter and height will also work. Both must be pressed firmly into the soil. This prevents the cutworm from reaching the tender stem. Once the plant grows larger, the stem grows tougher and is usually safe from serious damage.

That won't work on vegetables that are sown in rows like carrots and beets.

No it won't. The only control that I know of in that situation is chemical — diazinon granules sprinkled along the row at seeding or shortly after.

Cutworms are a nocturnal insect about 2.5 cm (1 in) long. They are brownish black in colour, so are camouflaged almost perfectly in soil. Plants cut off at or near the soil line are a sure (and often only) sign of their presence.

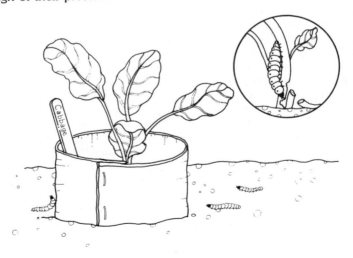

Tar paper prevention of cutworms
A tar paper collar around seedlings will stop the cutworms from reaching the stem.

92

Root Maggots

When I pulled up my turnips this year, they had little shallow tunnels all over the surface. What caused this?

This damage was probably caused by a white root maggot. The 5 mm (1/4 in) maggot hatches from eggs laid right beside the plants by a black fly slightly smaller than a house fly. They can winter over in the pupa stage in the soil and hatch out in the spring. So diazinon granules sprinkled in the row with the seeds at planting will control the maggots. This may have to be repeated in two to three weeks and sown along each side of the row in late August and early September.

I don't like using a lot of chemicals. Is there any other method of control?

There is a non-chemical control for root maggots similar to the method used for cutworms. In this case, you make a 10 cm × 10 cm (4 in × 4 in) tar paper collar with a hole just large enough to go around the stem of the plant and slit from the hole to the outside. This is placed around the stem at transplanting. It prevents the tiny fly, the adult stage of the maggot, from laying eggs next to the stem. The collar must be tight-fitting. Sometimes it's helpful to put a stone over the slit to prevent entry if the tar paper curls up. A light-weight tar paper used in built-up roofs does the job nicely.

The root or cabbage maggot is a serious pest of cabbage, cauliflower, Brussels sprouts, broccoli, celery, beets and radishes. Similar maggots attack onions. Root maggots can do enough damage to onions and radishes to ruin the bulbs and cause yellowing, wilting, and eventually destroy the plant. Stunted and wilting cabbage, cauliflower, broccoli or Brussels sprouts planted in May or early June should be examined by scratching around where the roots join the stem.

Because cool, wet weather favours the production of both cutworms and root maggots, they are at their peak of destructiveness in May and early June. Later seeding after early or mid-June in the cooler areas will avoid the early infestation which does the most damage. The damage from the later generation which occurs in late August and early September can be pared off the root crops just before cooking. You can also try moving the affected plants to another part of the garden, but avoid planting them near any of the other host plants mentioned.

Slugs and Snails

Slugs have invaded my garden. They are attacking my tomatoes and after a rain the whole garden is swarming with them.

Poison bait containing mataldehyde can be used to attract and kill slugs. Teaspoon-lots of bait should be moistened or placed in moist soil at the rate of one teaspoon per square metre (39 in × 39 in).

I have a pet dog that sniffs around the garden a lot. Is the bait poisonous to animals?

Yes, the bait is both attractive and poisonous to dogs and birds, so cover it loosely with a shingle or piece of board. While some manufacturers recommend scattering the bait, I would not recommend this because of the possibility of poisoning birds. The bait must also not come in contact with edible fruit and vegetables.

How long will the bait be effective once I put it on the soil?

While moisture is required to activate the bait, heavy rain leaches out the mataldehyde . Check bait piles after rain and, rain or shine, renew it on a weekly basis until the infestation is controlled.

Slugs and snails have been around for a long time. The common garden slug has been known to survive in captivity for almost a decade. Most species winter over as eggs but in the warm, wet coastal regions, they remain active year-round. They deposit eggs in moist areas. Full development from the egg stage takes almost a year or more depending on habitat and species.

Slugs are a persistent pest, so control measures must be equally persistent. First, review your watering practices. Slugs must have a rather consistently moist environment to thrive. In rainy parts of the country such as the west coast of British Columbia, nature favours the slug and eradication is difficult. In the parts of the country where watering is required during the summer months, it is possible to cut down on the slug population by watering as infrequently as possible. When you water, water with a sprinkler for hours, not minutes. To check that the watering is complete, dig down with a spade to make certain you have penetrated at least 15 cm (6 in). This could put as much time as two to three weeks between waterings in hot dry weather. The foliage and exposed soil surface will be powder dry. This makes life very difficult for the slug whose theme song is "Slip Sliding Along!"

Mulches benefit plants by conserving moisture. For that reason they favour the life cycle of the slug. The use of mulches may have to be curtailed until the slugs are cleaned up.

Whitefly Control

What can I use to control whitefly on edible crops such as parsley and mint? I also have tomatoes in a hydroponic unit under lights that are being attacked.

Chemical control using malathion is the usual recommendation provided that you do not harvest for twenty-four hours after application.

I tried malathion but it didn't seem to work.

Another insecticide recommended contains the active ingredient of methoxychlor but you must not harvest for three days after application. Rotenone and endosulfan, allowing two days without harvest, have also been known to be effective. Bear in mind that whitefly is an extremely persistent insect. Chemical control is difficult at best, because only the adults can be controlled. Whitefly has a four-stage life cycle that takes from twenty-one to twenty-eight days to complete depending on the temperature. My best advice then is to apply insecticide on five-to-seven day intervals for at least four applications. Hanging a Vapona No-Pest strip in an indoor situation can also reduce populations.

While a minor infestation of whitefly outdoors can be tolerated without taking action, a high population can cause plants to wither and die. The sticky honeydew excreted by the insect encourages the growth of sooty mould, further disfiguring the host plant. The adults are about 2 mm (1/16 in) long and have powdery white wings. They feed and lay eggs on the undersurface of young leaves. The eggs are pale yellow at first, but turn gray before hatching in five to seven days. The small white "crawlers" move around on the leaves for one or two days, then stay in one place to feed. Nymphs develop fully in two weeks at normal temperatures. The pupae are slightly larger and thicker than the nymphs. The adults emerge in about ten days. The complete life cycle takes four weeks.

There are presently two non-chemical control measures that have been proven to be successful. Scientists at the United States Department of Agriculture in Beltsville, Maryland discovered that whiteflies are attracted to the colour yellow. Specifically they used Rustoleum 659 Yellow but believe that other deep orange-yellow paints would be effective. The paint was applied to a 30 cm × 30 cm (12 in × 12 in) piece of light plywood which was then coated with SAE 90 motor oil. The boards were hung about 1 1/2 m (5 ft) apart among the host plants. The adult flying stage of whitefly was attracted to the boards and stuck like iron filings to a magnet. To avoid a messy contact of whitefly hunter and the oiled yellow boards, a wire screen can be placed around them.

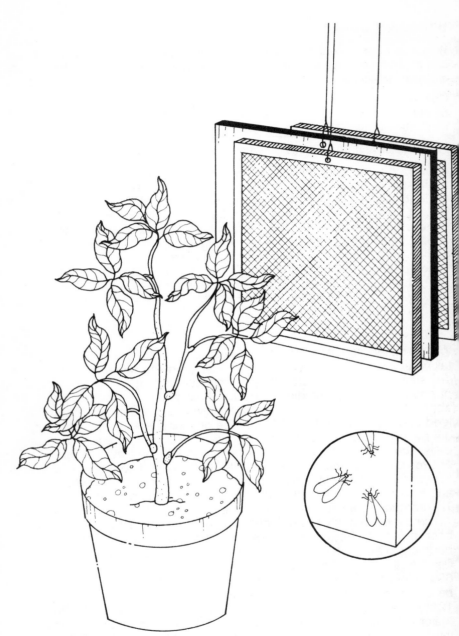

Whitefly trap
Yellow boards coated with heavy motor oil are hung between the plants.
The flies are attracted to the yellow colour and stick to the oil. A wire
screen can be placed around the boards.

Occasionally, you have the job of wiping the flies off with a paper towel and reapplying the oil. Controlled experiments indicated that 25 per cent of the whitefly population was attracted to the boards each twenty-four hour period. In another experiment complete control of adult white fly was effected in forty-eight hours.

European entomologists have pioneered in the biological control of whitefly. They discovered that a control program integrating a lethal parasitic wasp, *Encarsia formosa*, with the whitefly life cycle gave an excellent measure of control. The key word here though is "integrated." If all other measures fail, write: Information Division, Canada Department of Agriculture, Ottawa, Ontario, K1A 0C7. Ask for Bulletin 1469, "Integrated Control of the Greenhouse Whitefly." Carefully study the rather complex procedure to see if your situation requires biological control.

Finally, an exception to the rule. Normally fungicides only control specific fungus problems and have no effect on insects. Whitefly is the exception. It has been found that the nymph stage of whitefly can be controlled reasonably well with the fungicide maneb with the additional benefit of controlling some leaf diseases. Again, apply weekly for four weeks.

Currant Fruit Flies

I have a couple of red currant bushes. Last year a lot of berries dropped off before they were ready to be picked.

Did this happen early in the life of the berry?

Not really. They dropped throughout the development, some almost at maturity.

Then you have had proper pollination of the flower to set fruit. Are there spots on the berries?

Yes. There are dark red ones that have a reddish colour around them.

Then this is likely the work of the larva of the currant fruit fly. The insecticides recommended are malathion, methoxychlor, or rotenone. Apply when 80 per cent of the blossoms have withered and fallen and then again in ten days. This controls the adult fly before it lays eggs in the fruit.

Is there anything else I can do besides applying insecticide?

Disposing of the fruit as soon as it falls and before the larvae move out into the soil helps break the life cycle of the insect. Cultivating around the berry bushes may destroy pupae as well.

Currant fruit flies *(Epochra canadensis)* are found throughout Canada. The adult fly is 1 cm (1/3 in) long, yellow-bodied with darker shadings and conspicuously banded wings. The insect hibernates over winter in pupal stage in the soil. The adult hatches in the spring and lays eggs under the skin of currant and gooseberry berries. When the larvae hatch out they feed on the fruit, causing them to fall. They continue to feed for a few days on the ground, then enter the soil and go into the pupal state.

Timing is critical in the control of this insect because there is no control measure once the adult has laid the eggs in the fruit. Control of the adult fly must be effected before egg laying.

Leaf Roller on Fruit Trees

We have an apple tree that has just started to bloom, but the leaves are curled up and something is eating pieces out of them.

This sounds to me like the damage caused by the fruit tree leaf roller. The larva of this insect provides its own cover from predators by rolling up a leaf, binding it together with silk. Although the leaf damage may or may not be severe, it can bind a leaf around an emerging fruit bud or the fruit itself and do considerable damage. The best control is obtained by spraying with an insecticide or combination of insecticides containing the active ingredient of methoxychlor. Insecticides with the active ingredients of phosalone, carbaryl and phosmet should also be effective.

Fruit tree leaf roller *(Archips argyrospilus)*, although primarily known to attack apple trees, can injure all fruit trees and some ornamental in Canada and the northern half of the United States. The larva, th destructive stage of the insect, appears as leaves and fruit bud open. The slender, pale-green larva reaches alength of 2 cm (3/ in), entering the pupa stage in a folded leaf in June. Infestation ca be severe enough to destroy emerging flowers, prevent fruit set c seriously damage emerging fruit. The leaf damage may be sligh or severe.

About two weeks after formation, the pupa hatches into a brow 3 to 5 cm (1 to 2 in) moth with lighter markings on the front wing: The moth lays masses of eggs on the bark of twigs and branche secreting a substance which hardens to protect the eggs. The inse winters over at this stage, hatching the next year as the buds beg to open.

Like the professional orchardists, the home owner should follo a preventative spray schedule on fruit trees. Government bulletir (see page 145) outline such schedules, as do the containers domestic fruit tree sprays.

Peach Tree Borers

I have a peach tree that is bleeding large globs of sap near the base of the trunk.

Is there also sawdust, either mixed with the sap or separate?

Yes.

I believe your tree is being attacked by peach tree borers. These can only be controlled as the larvae are hatched out from the eggs laid in crevasses in the bark of the tree. This hatching can occur from late June through August. The insecticide that is recommended to control borers contains the active ingredient of endosulfan. Spray all bark thoroughly from the base to lower branches in late June, mid-July and early August.

Is there any non-chemical way of controlling the insect?

Once the larva eats its way under the bark the only way you may be able to destroy them is to clear congealed sap away from the holes. Then insert a flexible wire to try to impale the borer. Keeping the tree trunk covered from ground level to branches with strong paper such as masking tape, renewing as necessary, is another non-chemical control measure.

While a young, healthy tree can withstand a minor infestation of borers, unless they are brought under control the tree will soon be destroyed. The tree dies because the borer destroys the sap-conducting (cambium) tissue, effectively girdling or choking the tree. Because the incubation period from eggs to larvae can occur any time from late June through August, repeated sprayings are required. The insect winters over in the larva stage in burrows at the base of the infested tree. In the spring they complete their growth to a length of about 3 cm (1 in); then spin tough silken cocoons usually mixed with sawdust and soil particles. These can be found about 3 cm (1 in) below the soil surface any time from early June to September.

The moth which emerges between June and October can be mistaken for a wasp. It is clear-winged, steel-blue with yellow or orange markings. There are several yellow bands on the abdomen. The female's forewings are covered with metallic blue scales with the abdomen having a broad yellow band. There is only one generation per year. The clearest indication of the borer is the presence of gum mixed with sawdust.

The peach tree borer also attacks plums, cherry, almonds, apricot and nectarine, but the main target is peach trees.

Insect Damage on Raspberries

I have noticed that a fair number of my raspberry canes are bending over sharply near the tips. The tip then wilts and dies.

I believe the damage is caused by the adult of the raspberry cane borer. It is a slender, black beetle about 1 cm (1/2 in) long with prominent antennae. The neck of the beetle is yellow and the body black. The damage to the stem is caused by the insect's unusual procedure when it lays its egg. The beetle cuts two rings around the stem and lays its egg in the tissue between the rings. The cuts are sufficiently deep to cause the top 10 to 20 cm (4 to 8 in) of the stem to bend over and die. The egg hatches out into a yellowish grub which bores a little way down the stem and winters over there. Next year, it may kill the cane by boring all the way down. However, they don't usually attack that many canes.

What is the control measure then?

Cut off the stem just below where it is bent over and destroy it, killing the egg. July is the normal time the damage occurs. The damage is minimal and does not warrant chemical control.

SAP BEETLES are another pest of raspberries that have no chemical control. These are 5 mm (3/16 in) long black beetles with cream coloured markings. They can enter the fruit if you sit a box of it on the ground or will burrow into ripe fruit still on the cane. The population of sap beetles varies from year to year but every berry has to be examined when the population is high. Baiting is the only real control with a mixture of 900 g (2 lb) of crushed bananas or immature corn to 142 mL (5 oz) of 5.2 per cent endosulfan. Place about 11.3 g (1/4 lb) in an aluminum pie plate and cover with another pie plate punctured with 5 mm (3/16 in) holes. A small stone may be required to hold the perforated plate in place. Place the plates at 5 m (16 ft) intervals. Renew the bait weekly. Keep the bait out of the reach of children and pets. If in doubt about this, do not use endosulfan in the bait. Just dispose of the used bait and live sap beetles in the garbage.

FRUITWORMS damage raspberry plants in several ways. The very small beetles skeletonize young unfolding leaves, destroy blossom clusters and eat holes in blossom buds. Small larvae feed inside flower buds and in developing fruit. If this insect is a problem, spray or dust the plants with malathion and rotenone just before bloom. To protect bees, do not apply malathion during bloom.

RASPBERRY SAWFLY larvae are pale green and about 1 cm (1/2 in) long when full-grown. It is difficult to see the larvae but large irregular holes in the leaves are typical of this insect. The damage to the plants is usually not harmful. Treat the foliage with malathion and rotenone if it is severe. Again, do not apply malathion during bloom.

Wormy Apples

I have a McIntosh apple tree that is about twelve years old. We get an excellent crop but each year the apples are damaged by maggots. I use a spray containing ferbam and phosalone.

Ferbam is a fungicide which should control apple scab fungus. Phosalone is the insecticide and usually it will control apple maggot if applied at the right time.

Do you mean the timing of the spray is important?

Very important. The damage to the surface of the apple occurs when the adult, a 1 cm (1/2 in) dark brown fly, punctures the skin and lays tiny white eggs underneath. To control the maggots, you must kill the fly before it lays the eggs. Once the eggs are laid, there is no way to control the hatching of the 5 mm (1/4 in) maggot which mines the flesh of the apple, causing winding brown tunnels. The surface of the fruit becomes bumpy and dimpled. Many of the apples drop before maturity.

I'm not sure that's the problem I have. Are there any other insects that get into apples?

Yes, there are two other burrowing pests that can cause sufficient damage to ruin the fruit: the apple curculio and the codling moth. The adult of the curculio, a 1 cm (1/2 in) long weevil, breaks the surface of the apple in May or June, laying eggs in the flesh. A crescent-shaped, depressed scar develops on the fruit. White larvae hatch and tunnel in the fruit causing it to drop prematurely. It will also attack pear, plum and cherry in the same manner. The adult weevil must be controlled before it lays its eggs in the fruit by spraying with one of the carbaryl, methoxychlor, phosalone or phosmet. The spray must be applied when the fruit is 6 mm (1/4 in) in diameter and again ten days later. Carbaryl will sometimes cause fruit drop on apples. Codling moths lay eggs on the fruit, leaves and twigs of apples and pears from mid-June until mid-August. The larvae hatch, and tunnel in the fruit. Dark brown sawdust-like material is evident at the entry hole. Fruit often drops prematurely. There can be almost three complete generations per year necessitating a long control period.

Goodness, I think I may have all three pests. Is there any way I can control them and still use a minimum of insecticides?

Yes. The chemical controls for codling moth and apple maggot are similar. Part of your problem may come from unsprayed neighbourhood crabapple, hawthorn, prune or quince trees. Almost invariably these trees are not sprayed and act as a perpetual hatchery for all three of the insects we have been discussing. Control is extremely difficult under these conditions. Spray programs have been developed which offer a much higher chance of success than if you follow a haphazard schedule.

Some gardens seem to have little need of insecticides and fungicides to produce acceptable quality fruit. Others, like our questioner, are swamped with bugs and diseases and must follow an enlightened, properly timed spray program if they are to eat any fruit of their labours. On the following pages are spray programs for fruit trees showing the choice of active ingredients to control disease and insects plus the timing of the sprays. The chemical recommendations are for Ontario. Not all these chemicals may be registered in all provinces for domestic use. Use only those that are, carefully observing the time of the last spray before harvest on each product label. It is an important part of the control of apple maggot and curculio to gather and dispose of the fallen apples as they drop. This prevents the maggots leaving the apple and hibernating as pupae in the soil and on debris.

SPRAY PROGRAM FOR APPLE AND PEAR

TIME TO SPRAY	PESTS TO CONTROL	PESTICIDES TO USE	REMARKS
Dormant stage (before buds break)	Scale insects Mites	Use one of: dormant oil sprays lime sulphur	Spray before buds break; use sufficient spray mixture to cover all parts of tree thoroughly and spray from all sides. Dormant oil may cause bark of Red Delicious apple trees to become abnormal. Spray dormant oil in the morning to allow thorough drying before a cold night.
When buds break until open flower bud cluster	Scab	Use one of: benomyl captan ferbam sulphur	Sprays may be required weekly during this time if prolonged wet periods occur. Do not apply captan if dormant spray oil was applied. Do not use benomyl on pear.
From pink flower buds until first open blossoms	Scab Caterpillars Pear psylla	Same as above Add one of: carbaryl diazinon methoxychlor phosmet phosalone	Do not use methoxychlor for pear psylla. If aphids become a problem, use either the diazinon or phosalone. Never use insecticides when blossoms open or dandelions are in bloom under fruit trees.

TIME TO SPRAY	PESTS TO CONTROL	PESTICIDES TO USE	REMARKS
Blossom period	DO NOT APPLY INSECTICIDES OR MULTIPURPOSE MIXTURES DURING BLOSSOM PERIOD		A spray of captan or benomyl may be applied for scab if necessary. Do not use benomyl on pear.
When flower petals fall	Scab	Use one of: benomyl captan ferbam sulphur	If mites have been a serious problem use dimethoate, phosalone or a mixture containing dicofol. Carbaryl insecticide causes thinning of apples (not pears) and should not be used at this time. Do not use benomyl on pear.
	Pear psylla Curculio Plant bugs Mites	Add one of: diazinon dimethoate phosalone phosmet	
12 days after petals fall and repeat at 12- to 14-day intervals until about mid-August	Scab	Use one of: benomyl captan ferbam sulphur	*Observe no-spray interval before harvest as stated on product label.* Do not use benomyl on pear.
	Pear psylla Curculio Apple maggot Codling moth	Add one of: carbaryl diazinon dimethoate phosalone phosmet	Unless fruit set on apple is very heavy, do not use carbaryl insecticide within 3 weeks after petals fall. Apple maggot is very difficult to control if unsprayed apple, crabapple, prune, quince or hawthorn trees grow nearby.

SPRAY PROGRAM FOR PEACH, PLUM AND CHERRY

TIME TO SPRAY	PESTS TO CONTROL	PESTICIDES TO USE	REMARKS
Dormant stage (before buds break)	Scale insects Mites	Use one of: dormant oil spray lime sulphur	Spray dormant oil in the morning to allow thorough drying before a cold night. One spray for peach leaf curl is usually needed every year.
	Peach leaf curl	Use one of: ferbam lime sulphur	
When flower petals fall	Leaf spot Brown rot	Use one of: benomyl captan ferbam sulphur	Leaf spot is not a problem on peach. On plum and cherry, use captan or ferbam if leaf spot is serious. Do not use phosmet on sweet cherry. Spray immediately when petals start to fall.
	Curculio	Add one of: carbaryl diazinon phosalone phosmet	
10 days later	Leaf spot Brown rot	Same as above	
	Curculio	Same as above	
July 1-10	Leaf spot Brown rot	Use one of: benomyl captan ferbam sulfur	Dates for this and following sprays are only approximate, depending on geographic location. Where cherry maggot has been a problem in previous year, also spray 10 days earlier (June 20-30). Do not apply phosmet on sweet cherry. Dimethoate may only be used on sweet and sour cherries.
	Cherry maggot Fruit moth worms in peach	Add one of: carbaryl diazinon dimethoate phosalone phosmet	

TIME TO SPRAY	PESTS TO CONTROL	PESTICIDES TO USE	REMARKS
July 15-30	Leaf spot Brown rot	Same as above	*Observe no-spray interval before harvest as stated on product label.* Check foliage at this time for mite injury.
	Worms in peach Maggots in prune	Same as above (except dimethoate)	
Later sprays	Leaf spot Brown rot	Same as above	On cherry, apply only fungicide for leaf spot after harvest. Late peaches may require an insecticide about 4 weeks before picking. Plums and peaches may require an extra spray for brown rot before harvest. *Observe no-spray interval before harvest as stated on product label.*
	Worms in peach	Same as above (except dimethoate)	

Rodent Deterrents

I have a family of Mama and Papa groundhog and offspring that are the healthiest I have ever seen. They are having the grandest time in my vegetable patch. I don't want to kill them but do you know how to get rid of them?

Some humane societies rent out live animal traps. When baited correctly, these trap the animal alive. They can then be released where they will do no damage. To buy, and they are available, such a trap costs about $50.00.*

I just want them to stay out of my garden.

Another way to discourage them is to lay a continuous narrow stream of blood meal, an organic fertilizer, around the edge of the garden. Some gardeners claim the smell keeps rodents away. You could also try a similar barrier of finely powdered sulphur** (orchard spray sulphur powder), available from garden centres and farm supply dealers.

The method you use to control groundhogs and other rodents depends on your attitude toward them. As a boy on our market garden, groundhogs were "taken care of" by a faithful collie dog. Whether or not he sensed that when groundhogs got the cabbage they destroyed his master's livelihood, I don't know. But he went after them with cunning zeal. He would observe their territory and habits from afar and calculate the best strategy that put him between the groundhog and his hole while the groundhog was the furthest distance from it. He seldom miscalculated. As long as we had Sootie we knew the groundhogs were taken care of.

If you decide that you deserve the fruits of your labour and that thieves are thieves whether they wear a fur coat in the summer or not, then there are gas cartridges that dispatch groundhogs painlessly. All the holes must be discovered and filled with soil. Before the last one is filled, a sulphur oxide*** cartridge is ignited and dropped into the hole.

---

*Available from: Kathleen Wilson, 58 Edgar Avenue, Thornhill, Ontario, L4J 1S6
**Manufactured by: Chipiman Chemicals, Stoney Creek, Ontario, (Microfine Sulphur 92)
***Also available at garden centres and farm supply dealers. Manufactured by: Sanex Chemicals Ltd.,6490 Bombardier St., Montreal, Quebec, H1P 1E2

Coon-Trol

I am plagued with those animal bandits called coons. They get my corn every time.

I have had several control methods forwarded by listeners to Radio Noon. One is to drive small stakes 60 cm (24 in) high at frequent intervals throughout the garden. To the top of the stake, tack a 15 cm × 15 cm (6 in × 6 in) piece of cloth that has been soaked in creolin disinfectant. This will deter coons, fox, rabbits and dogs. If you are losing fowl as well, a little creolin brushed on the large tail feathers will turn away predators.

Another method that is purported to be foolproof is to light and leave burning overnight, small truck flares that burn kerosene. Either the flickering flame or the kerosene smell or both keep coons at bay.

With corn, a small paper bag placed over each cob as they form will usually keep the cob unharmed.

You also have the option of live trapping (page 107).

Mole-Trol

My garden and rockery are riddled with moles. They are eating my bulbs and root crops.

Even an aggressive cat has trouble controlling moles. Listeners to Radio Noon have offered two methods that they claim are effective. One involves the use of a 4 or 6 quart basket. The handle is removed and two 4 cm (1 1/2 in) holes are cut in each end of the basket just above the bottom of the basket. A shallow, 2.5 cm (1 in) high open-top carton is tacked to the floor of the basket. This could be the cut off bottom of a breakfast cereal box. Place a good poison mouse bait in the carton and sit the basket on the mole runs. Cover it with a waterproof lid and weight with a stone so that only the moles have access to the poison through the holes. A shallow bowl of water nearby seems to make the bait more effective. You can operate as many of these mole control centres as you need.

Is there anything I can do that doesn't involve poisoning them?

Another method is to dig down into mole tunnels, opening up a small section of the tunnel. Place 28 mL (2 tblsp) of moth crystals (paradichlorobenzine) in the tunnel. Cover the excavation with a small piece of plywood and soil. Repeat this procedure at 2 m (6 ft) intervals wherever you can find mole tunnels. The fumes will circulate through the tunnels and drive away the moles. Moth balls will not work.

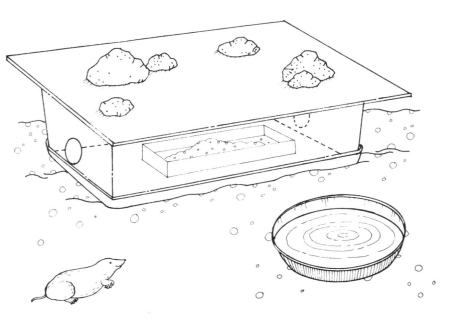

Mole bait

This mole bait makes use of a 4 or 6 quart basket baited with mouse poison. A saucer of water nearby seems to help attract the moles.

Chapter 6: Weeds and Diseases

Preventing Weeds in a Vegetable Garden

What is the easiest way of keeping weeds out of a vegetable garden?

If you are using transplants such as tomatoes, you can use a chemical weed preventer containing chlorthal or trifluralin.* This kills germinating weed seeds of many different species. You can also use a herbicide containing paraquat diquat between the rows.

What about using mulches?

Any non-toxic material that prevents light from getting to the soil will prevent the germination and growth of weeds. Newspaper, black plastic, no-weed plastic mulch, peat moss and cocoa bean shells will all work.

The most common and still satisfactory weed preventer is cultivation. The important thing is timing. Most weeds are very easy to kill if disturbed by cultivation on a bright, breezy day provided they are in the process of, or have recently, germinated. Even if you can't see the weeds, light cultivation will knock out 95 per cent of them before they become a nuisance. Don't wait until they are 5 to 10 cm (2 to 4 in) high before attacking them. Prompt cultivation soon after a rainfall or watering will take most of the back-break out of weeding.

Chemical weed preventers containing 75 per cent chlorthal can be sprayed on and around most vegetable plants (exceptions will be noted on the container) after all existing weeds are cleaned up. Chlorthal or trifluralin do not control weeds after they have emerged. It is most effective sprayed or dusted on the soil prior to transplanting. As it destroys all germinating seeds, it cannot be used where you sow seeds of most vegetables. It gives good control for about three months.

A herbicide containing paraquat diquat kills anything green and must only be applied between the rows, on a still day with a coarse spray to prevent any drift to desirable plant material. The foliage sprayed must not be ingested. It is highly toxic but once it comes in contact with the soil, it goes inert.

A University of Toronto scientist has recently developed a material called ecolyte. When added to polyethylene plastic film, it causes the film to break down into a fine ash after about a ninety-day exposure to sunlight. A no-weed plastic mulch containing ecolyte is available at most garden centres. Installed prior to planting, it

*Check the label for species on which it has been safely used.

prevents weed germination for the whole growing season and dissolves into ash, eliminating any disposal problem.

On heat-loving crops sucn as tomatoes, cucumbers, melons, squash, peppers and beans, no-weed mulches increase soil temperature, hastening maturity and increasing production. No cultivation is necessary and no chemicals need be applied. Because the soil is not exposed to air movement, no-weed plastic mulch is a great conserver of water and allows the plant to have active roots close to the surface of the soil without being disturbed by cultivation.

It takes time to apply the plastic mulch, but once it is done weeding is all but eliminated, watering is reduced, productivity increased and maturity hastened.

Peat moss as a weed preventive mulch is also effective, as are cocoa bean shells. Both can later be incorporated into the soil to benefit the next year's crop.

Caution: Paraquat Diquat is a toxic material. Care should be taken during application to avoid skin contact. Wear rubber gloves. While the herbicide goes inert with contact with soil, foliage sprayed with the chemical is toxic to man and beast.

Removing Twitch Grass from an Asparagus Bed

I would like to know how to remove twitch grass from an asparagus bed.

During the cutting season you can use a herbicide containing paraquat diquat which kills anything green. This is a contact herbicide which does not translocate within the plant and therefore does not kill the root system. However if you repeat the spray of paraquat diquat each time new growth appears you can bring twitch under control (see warning). In addition to killing the twitch, it will destroy all other weeds wherever applied.

Won't it hurt the asparagus?

All the asparagus spears, every tip visible, must be cut off prior to spraying. Paraquat diquat does not harm root systems and it goes inert when it comes in contact with soil.

Twitch grass is a very aggressive, persistent, perennial grass. It propagates itself both from seed and more relentlessly from its root system. Twitch is a broader bladed grass than ornamental lawn grasses with blades emerging straight up, then unrolling and flattening out to a 5 mm (1/4 in) width. Successive blades emerge from

111

a central growing point until at maturity (the height varies with the growing conditions) a seed stalk emerges.

Twitch is probably more readily identified by its aggressive rhizome root system which sends 3 to 4 mm (1/8 in) white spears off horizontally in all directions. While asparagus will actually survive with grasses, the competition from the grass decimates the production. For this reason, the twitch must be controlled.

Before the advent of herbicides, the only method of control was a digging fork, a bushel basket and a strong back. The root system of the grass is generally confined to the top 10 cm (4 in) of the soil and digging and shaking out the roots will physically remove it. However, 2 cm (3/4 in) of white roots missed in this digging operation will soon generate new growth. Only digging out the roots meticulously will work. I have spent many a warm June Saturday, as a boy, doing just that.

You cannot cultivate over the crowns of the asparagus during the growing season without destroying the emerging spears so cultivation to eliminate twitch in asparagus is ineffective.

Black Walnut Toxicity

I wanted to plant a black walnut in my yard. Is there any truth to the idea that some plants won't grow near a black walnut?

The roots of black walnut contain a toxic substance called juglone. This will kill many species of plants including potatoes and tomatoes. Juglone is not secreted into the soil. There must be contact between the roots of the affected species and the black walnut.

How far does this toxic zone reach?

It extends as far as the roots. Injury has been observed as far as 24 m (80 ft) from the trunk of a mature black walnut. The toxin in the roots persists long after a black walnut is cut down, presumably until the root system rots and disappears. Injury is sometimes sporadic. With plants of the same species within the general root area of the black walnut, some are injured, some may not be injured.

Is there anything you can do to prevent injury?

No. Heavy leaching with water does not help. Black walnut is a valuable tree where it can be given a wide birth, but I would not plant it on an urban lot.

Potato Scab and Wood Ashes

I have quite a few wood ashes each year. I understand that they are good for the garden but can cause scab on potatoes.

Wood ashes do contain beneficial amounts of potash, a major chemical element required for plant growth. However, they also contain sodium and calcium hydroxides which are alkaline and raise the pH of the soil. The pH is the measure of alkalinity or acidity. A reading of 7.0 is neutral — below 7.0 is acidic, above is alkaline. Scab fungus thrives in a near neutral or alkaline soil. So if you want to avoid potato scab, I would not apply wood ashes directly to the soil where potatoes will be grown.

With more and more woodburning stoves and fireplaces coming into use, the disposal of wood ashes becomes a greater challenge. One of the best ways to use ashes is by way of the compost heap. Composting requires an acid neutralizer, and in Chapter One we recommend agricultural limestone. Wood ashes could be a logical substitute, enriching the compost with potash and other beneficial elements.

The effect of wood ashes on potatoes explains why farmers seldom apply lime to potato soils prior to planting. The potatoes would probably grow better in the higher pH (less acid) soil, but the danger of creating an ideal environment for the growth of disfiguring potato scab is always present in a near-alkaline soil. The disease seldom occurs in soils where the pH is 5.0 or lower and may occur with great severity in a soil with a pH of 6.0 and above.

A complete soil test or at least a pH test is the only accurate way of determining pH (see pages 17 to 18). If you are having trouble with potato scab and a soil test indicates a high pH, then you can lower the pH with sphagnum peat. It will take approximately 10 to 15 cm (4 to 6 in) of sphagnum peat moss worked into the top 15 to 20 cm (6 to 8 in) of a sandy or sandy loam soil to lower the pH reading by one point. Sulphur applied at the rate of 340 to 680 g per 9 m² (3/4 to 1 1/2 lb per 100 ft²) will also lower the pH one point.

Potato scab first appears as minute reddish-brown lesions around the breathing pores on small tubers. They soon increase in size, become dark and form circular scab areas which, under severe infestation, cover the whole potato. While the potato is still edible, deep paring is required to eliminate the scab.

The organism will winter over on potato debris or in the soil. Manure applied to the soil also favours potato scab. One of the most effective ways of controlling scab is to plant resistant potato varieties such as Avon, Netted Gem, Cherokee and Sebago.

Black Currants and Pine Trees

When I bought this new property years ago, I had a garden alongside some pine trees. My currant bushes growing there would never bear fruit. I was told that pine trees affected currants and I might as well rip them out. Do you agree?

Did the pine trees shade the currants?

No, they were some distance away; far enough that I am sure the roots of the pine were not interfering.

The problem with currants and pine trees is not that the pines would directly affect the fruiting of currants but that pine tree rust lives out part of its life on pine trees and part on currants. This is a fungus disease which on the currant appears as orange spots which later develop into pimples on the lower surface of the leaves. It affects all currants but will only defoliate black currants. It may kill white pines after many years of infection. For this reason, parts of the United States ban the growing of currants and follow eradication programs of all currants. A similar problem exists between wheat and barberry. It is illegal to propagate, import or sell barberry in Canada because it acts as a host for wheat rust. The same step has not been taken in Canada with currants. The rust fungus can be controlled with lime sulphur sprayed just before bloom and again after harvest.

Currants Defoliate Prematurely

We have a very persistent problem with mildew on our currant bushes. We hardly dare harvest the currants because of the all-purpose chemical my husband uses. They start growing well but then the leaves begin to curl, turn yellow and fall off.

I don't believe what you are describing is mildew. It sounds more like the damage that leaf spot can do on currants. You spoke of an all-purpose chemical. Keep in mind that garden spray and dust chemicals come in two broad categories: fungicides which control certain fungus disease problems, and insecticides which control specified insects. You are dealing here with a fungus so a fungicide is called for. Any given fungicide will not control all fungus diseases. The fungicide package will list possible fungi controlled. So the first step is to determine what you are dealing with. Books, government bulletins or reputable nurseries that sell the chemicals should identify the disease, recommend both chemical and non-chemical control and, of equal importance, the timing of the control measures.

Then this chemical we have been applying may not even be a fungicide.

That is correct. The chemical fungicide for leaf spot involves lime sulphur, folpep, maneb or captan. Because the currant bushes have been heavily attacked in previous years, I would recommend you combine lime sulphur with either folpep, captan or maneb. Spray just before blossoms open, just after blossoming, again two weeks after this. Apply a fourth time after the fruit has been picked.

What about starting up another planting of currants in another spot in the garden?

The spores from these diseases winter over on debris and soil and are found on natural vegetation. They can be moved by the wind. When they land on a suitable host under the right conditions of moisture and temperature, they germinate. Moving to another location in the space provided by the average house garden would only provide very temporary respite, if any at all.

Leaf spot *(Anthracnose rubis)* causes very small brown circular spots first on the lower foliage. If the spots are numerous enough, the leaves turn yellow and fall from the bottom of the bush upward. It is an important part of control to rake up and burn all affected foliage.

Powdery mildew *(Sphaerotheca mors)* is a serious fungus disease particularly on black currant and gooseberry. Fruit will dry up with a brown, felty coating. Leaves and canes are stunted and will also have this felty coating. This has a pronounced effect on production. The control is similar to that for leaf spot except one earlier spray should be applied just as the leaf buds are breaking in the spring. The rest of the sprays for mildew have the same timing and chemicals as leaf spot, only substitute benomyl for maneb which is not effective against mildew.

Cut Flowers and Rot on Strawberries

I have had two problems with strawberries. When the blossoms were out I noticed a lot of blooms with partially cut stems. When I examined them closer some of the blossoms were brown and lifeless, although they weren't cut off. Others had tiny holes in them.

You are describing injury caused by a tiny 3 mm (1/8 in) bug called a clipper weevil. They are reddish-brown in colour and emerge as soon as growth starts in the spring. They can drastically reduce the yield. The control is to spray with malathion when the buds begin to open.

The other problem occurred later. A fairly large percentage of the fruit was soft and rotten just before or at maturity. If these were left

*on the plants, they went completely rotten and then little stems
covered with a dust appeared all over the fruit.*

That's an apt description of a fungus disease called botrytis as it goes
through its various stages of development. It may have begun in the
blossom stage, maturing along with the fruit and destroying it in the
process. Botrytis thrives in temperatures around 13°C (55°F) and
moisture. Narrow rows on ridges help prevent botrytis by
encouraging air movement, drying out the foliage quickly after dew
or rain. Always water early in the morning so that sun and wind dry
the leaves and blossoms quickly. Spraying with a combination of
benomyl and captan every two weeks between blossom and harvest
may be necessary. These chemicals can be combined with any
recommended insecticide in one spray if insects are a problem during
the same period. Be certain that the spray is strong enough to
penetrate the foliage, reaching blossoms and stems.

Brown Rot and Fireblight on Fruit Trees

*I have dark brown rot on my plum and cherry trees. I have been
told that I may have to have the trees destroyed.*

There are two different diseases which could cause the symptoms
you describe. One is brown rot, the other is fireblight. Because the
host trees are plum and cherry, the problem is most likely brown rot.
Brown rot is a fungus disease and can be controlled by fortnightly
sprays alternating benomyl with captan or as a second choice folpep
combined with lime sulphur as soon as the problem occurs. Next
season I would begin this spray program when the blossoms begin to
open. Captan and folpep are often included in the active ingredients
of multi-purpose fruit tree spray mixtures.

If you have ever tried to hold over a basket of peaches, plums or
cherries only to find them succumb to small brown spots which
appear to grow hourly until the whole fruit is ruined, you have a
basket case of the problem in question. However, if this is indeed
the culprit *(Sclerotinia fruiticola)* the tree itself need not be a basket
case. The initial invasion of brown rot turns the petals of the emerging
blossoms brown prematurely. They will rot in moist weather. This
may go unnoticed. Occasionally there is leaf and twig blight; cankers
can form on the larger branches, causing sap to seep out.

As the brown spots in the fruit enlarge, gray to light-brown spore
tufts appear. If left on the tree, the fruit mummifies, sometimes cling-
ing to the tree, sometimes falling off. All of this fruit should be gath-
ered and put in the garbage to prevent the disease from spreading
or lasting over the winter.

116

While the disease can be spread by means of blowing rain, it can also be carried by feeding insects. This is another good reason to follow a spray schedule if you are having this problem.

Brown rot, in order of likelihood, appears on peach, plum, cherry, apricot, almond, Japanese quince and rarely on apple and pear.

Fireblight (Erwinia amylovora) is most likely found on apple, crab-apple, pear and quince, and less frequently on almond, apricot, cherry, plum, raspberry and strawberry. Fireblight is a bacterial disease and is much more difficult to control. As with brown rot, blossoms are the first part of the tree to be affected and they turn black and shrivel. The disease spreads more quickly in warm, humid weather as it moves from blossoms to branches and leaves. Later young branches turn black.The bark is shrunken, dark-brown to purplish and sometimes blistered with gum oozing out. The dead leaves do not usually fall off but instead give the infected branch the appearance of having been scorched with fire. The bacteria survive the winter in the life tissue at the edge of the cankers. Fruit can also turn brown and rot.

The bacteria are most active in late spring and go dormant as weather gets hotter. Carefully remove the affected branches, cutting them at least 20 cm (8 in) below the infected parts. Dip the sheers in a mixture of one part chlorox to four parts water in between cuts to avoid the spreading of the bacteria. Bacteria are also spread by insects which should be carefully controlled with a regular spray program for fruit trees.

Fireblight bacteria are the most virulent in soft new growth. As this can be promoted by applications of nitrogen fertilizer, it is best not to apply nitrogen around trees in question until after blossoms are finished.

Spur Blight on Raspberries

I was pruning out my old raspberry canes right after the picking season, and noticed brownish-purple splotches on the stems of the new growth. Is this some kind of disease?

This is a fungus called spur blight, and occurs on new growth, usually around the leaf axils. It will kill the embryo spurs or branches which would normally grow and bear fruit. As much as 75 per cent of a crop can be destroyed. Summer pruning thins out the growth, increases air circulation and helps stop the fungus from spreading. The chemical control is to spray with lime sulphur just as the leaves are breaking bud in the spring. Follow up with a spray of captan when the new growth is 15 to 20 cm (6 to 8 in) long and again when this growth is 30 to 40 cm (12 to 15 in) long. Repeat two weeks later, spraying thoroughly to the point of spray run off each time.

This same spraying procedure will also help control anthracnose, another fungus disease. Anthracnose destroys the plant tissue on the canes, causing gray spots with purple borders. Later the bark may crack. If severe, the branches and leaves are affected, immature fruit dries up and mature fruit becomes soft and mushy. Fruit rot may also be caused by the fungus botrytis during a wet season. Captan or benomyl applied at the blooming period and then every ten days until maturity is the chemical control. It is safe to apply to within one day of harvest.

Blossom End Rot on Tomatoes

Last year I had a large black spot on the bottom end of my tomatoes. Usually it would end up rotten.

The problem is called blossom end rot. It can be caused by two factors. One is any weather factor (heat or hot dry wind) that causes the tomato blossom to wilt just as the embryo fruit is forming. This causes some cell damage which is magnified as the fruit develops. The other cause is insufficient calcium, which prevents proper cell structure.

How can I get calcium into the plant?

Calcium can be added when you prepare the soil in the form of ground limestone (calcium carbonate, agricultural lime) or ground dolmitic limestone which contains magnesium as well as calcium carbonate. Magnesium is one of the minor elements required for balanced plant growth.

Is there anything I can do when the plants are already in?

During the growing season, calcium is quickly available by fertilizing with water-soluble calcium nitrate at the rate of 10 mL per 5 litres (2 tblsp per gallon) of water.

Blossom end rot is usually a firm black sunken area on the tomato fruit. Occasionally a secondary fungus invades the affected area, causing a soft rot. It occurs most frequently after a rainfall to the earlier set of fruit. The moisture causes a surge of growth and if there is inadequate calcium available, the cells in the fruit are malformed. Wide fluctuations in moisture can cause wilting and contribute to the problem. Even moisture is important to control blossom end rot. Any form of mulch which helps retain moisture is of great benefit. (see pages 110 to 111).

Wilt Disease in Tomatoes

I plant my tomatoes in the same spot in my garden every year but last year they started wilting a branch at a time.

Do the leaves turn yellow and does the stem become brown and eventually soft?

Yes. The whole plant finally died.

The cause of the problem is likely verticillium or possibly fusarium wilt disease. The fungus winters over in the soil for two to four years and enters the plants through its roots. Moving your tomatoes to another place in the garden not contaminated by run-off water from the area of the disease is one solution. Another solution is to buy tomato varieties with a genetically built-in resistance to the disease.

How can I tell which varieties are resistant?

Good seed catalogues and plant labels at better nurseries indicate this by the letters VFN after the name. This indicates verticillium, fusarium and nematode (a tiny root-destroying insect) resistance.

Verticillium also attacks potatoes, peppers, eggplant, watermelons, cantaloupe, raspberries, strawberries, apricots, peaches and cherries, so do not plant these species in the infected area for a period of four years. The fungi, having entered the plant from the soil through the roots, causes the roots to go brown. Cutting through the stem of an infected plant will also reveal a brown discoloration in the sap-conducting tissue near the outer edge. The oldest leaves usually show the characteristic wilting symptom first. In the leaves, the symptoms are wilted, V-shaped yellow areas extending from the margins of the leaves.

Shelf Life of Pesticides and Herbicides

I have some pesticides that are two and three years old. Are they still safe to use and will they still work?

That all depends on how the chemicals have been stored. Most manufacturers void any warranty after the chemical is two years old. You should always keep the chemical in its original container, tightly sealed and out of sunlight. Store it in a well-ventilated place with the temperature above freezing and below 38°C (100°F). Store all powders above ground to avoid picking up moisture. Keep volatile herbicides (2-4-D, etc.) at least 3 m (10 ft) away from pesticides to avoid contamination of the pesticides. Never use the same spray equipment for pesticides and herbicides. Herbicides cannot be removed from sprayers by rinsing and washing.

Chapter 7: Growing Food Plants in Containers

Growing Transplants Indoors: Seeding and Transplanting

I want to start my vegetables indoors this year, from seed, and then transplant them into the garden. Can I just sow the seeds in regular pots, or what is the best kind of container to use?

I prefer plastic cell packs which fit into a plastic carrying tray. Most garden centres handle them and the trays have anywhere from 32 to 72 cells. The carrying tray is available with or without drainage holes. If yours is a window-sill growing operation, you may want the tray without holes to prevent drainage water from leaking out.

What's the best kind of soil to use?

We have germinated literally millions of seedlings in our time and the best media we have found to date is Peat-lite, an artificial soil consisting of peat, vermiculite and other additives. It is lightweight, sterile, and produces good root systems and vigorous growth. Pro-Mix and Redi-Earth are two brand names, but you can also mix Peat-lite yourself.*

Couldn't I use just regular potting soil?

Most other packaged potting soils do not drain rapidly enough. I would recommend you mix one part potting soil, one part sphagnum peat moss and one part vermiculite as an alternative to Peat-lite.

How warm can the room be that the seedlings are put in?

Room temperature — 21°C (70°F) — will work well for both germination and growing on immediately after transplanting. However, the last week or ten days prior to transplanting in the garden require outside conditions and lower temperatures to acclimate the plants.

Most vegetables** that are started from seeds sown indoors, should be sown in rows about 3 seeds per 1/2 cm (1/4 in) row with rows about 3 to 5 cm (1 to 2 in) apart. A plastic bedding plant container measuring 25 cm × 51 cm (10 in × 20 in) works well. The rows can be arranged across the narrow width or lengthwise, depending

---

*See *Plants: Answers That Work* by Ken Reeves for complete instructions.
**peppers, tomatoes, lettuce, cabbage, celery, Brussels sprouts and broccoli

on the number of seeds of each variety. Fewer seeds can be sown in individual pots or plastic containers of an appropriate size. All containers used should have a liberal number of drainage holes. The seedling media should be levelled and thoroughly moistened prior to seeding. The seeds of most vegetables are of sufficient size to warrant covering with seedling media (Peat-lite) to a depth of no more than twice the thickness of the seed. Water the container with a fine nozzle to moisten the covering.

A film of clear plastic can be stretched taut over the seedling container to prevent drying out. The plastic should be about 13 mm (1/2 in) above the surface of the seedling media to prevent the emerging seedling from sticking to the plastic sheet. It is critical that the media be kept uniformly moist until the seedling emerges. The plastic will have to be removed as soon as the earliest seeds sprout or severe stretching and spindly seedlings will result. In place of the plastic sheet, a new clear plastic hood is available for the tray. The same depth as the tray, it creates an excellent draft-free, humid environment for propagating cuttings and germinating seeds.

With the exception of cucumber, cantaloupe and onions most other vegetables benefit from transplanting and should be spaced out about 5 cm (2 in) apart when transplanted. This operation is best done when the seedlings have developed two or three sets of leaves. Plastic inserts that fit the 25 × 51 cm (10 in × 20 in) tray with individually formed cells ranging from 32 to 72 per insert work well — 5 cm (2 in) peat pots, plastic pots, 6 oz styrofoam coffee cups or transplanting into open trays will give the plants the individual space they need prior to their final transplanting into the garden.

Cucumbers, melons and squash are best sown directly into the individual 5 cm (2 in) cell or pot, two to four seeds per container with no further transplanting indoors. This clump of plants is then transplanted into the garden undisturbed.

To acclimate plants to outside conditions, move the plants outdoors when the temperature is above freezing. This exposes them to higher light, wind and lower temperatures. Watch them carefully for any sign of burning the first couple of days. A cold frame and removable sash is ideal for this operation, giving some protection but still allowing the plants to harden in preparation for the final move into the garden. The acclimating (hardening off) is extremely important to the success of your growing endeavour.

If you have plenty of light, you may find you can sow a week or two earlier. However, it is best to keep to a short schedule and end up with smaller, well acclimated seedlings than overgrown, spindly ones.

Growing Vegetables Indoors: Light Requirements

I have planted tomato seedlings indoors and I am concerned because the stems are so spindly.

I believe the problem is caused by insufficient light. To achieve stocky, vigorous growth tomatoes require much higher light levels than are available even in a south window in March and April.

Can I do anything now about the spindly stalks?

Yes. Put the seedlings right in an unobstructed south (preferably) or east or west window with no sheers, if possible a window where the temperature is about 15°C (59°F). Allow minor wilting between waterings.

Would I be better to put them under my fluorescent light units?

Possibly, if the bulbs can be suspended within 15 cm (6 in) of the ti of the plants and there are at least 4 tubes within a 30 cm (12 in) width to ensure maximum light for eighteen hours a day.

Growing your own vegetable transplants can be a rewarding ar challenging project. The factor that limits success is usually low lig levels. Remember that any window allows in light from one side on Picture a large cardboard carton sitting in your garden with only or side open to the south. A plant placed in that carton is going receive considerably less light than if it were out in the open. window has the same limitation of light.

Vegetable plants in general and tomatoes in particular are, t nature, full summer sun plants. They will tolerate less than this b it does affect their growth and productivity.

Artificial light, if it is in sufficient quantity, will help. To be specifi bright, working light for such tasks as accounting, sewing or dentist is in the order of 200 foot candles. To grow reasonable quality toma transplants requires 300 to 800 foot candles — very bright lig indeed. In addition, the seedlings must be very close to the lig source because light energy drops off in the ratio of the square the distance from the source. An object two feet from a light sourc receives only one fourth the energy that is avilable at the sourc This means that your seedling must be as close as possible to window or fluorescent fixture.

Fluorescent light is a good source of light for plant growing. M source of light for writing this book is the conventional incandesce desk lamp. I can feel the heat from the red rays of the incandesce bulbs 40 cm (16 in) from the bulb. Cool white fluorescent light h little of the red (heat) rays in the spectrum, so that plants can b placed very close to the bulbs for maximum growth energy, withc getting excessively hot.

If you are choosing fluorescent fixtures, keep in mind that they come in three different outputs: regular, high output, (HO) and very high output (VHO). All plants in general, and vegetable seedlings in particular, would benefit from the VHO tubes (HO and VHO must be used with fixtures designed for these outputs). Cool white bulbs have proven to be as effective as any other under laboratory testing conditions. The VHO lamps of course will take more watts of electricity but watts are what make plants grow.

Container-Grown Tomatoes: Varieties and Soil Requirements

I want to grow tomatoes on my balcony this summer. Are some varieties better for growing in pots than others?

Choosing a variety of tomato to grow in a container is even more important than choosing one to grow in the garden. This is where the shortcomings of line-bred or non-hybrid varieties show up. Good hybrids have vigorous disease-resistant attributes. My choice for our garden in Southern Ontario is Supersonic, Jetstar, Ultra Boy for beefsteak-type slicing tomatoes and Sweet 100 for cherry-sized fruit.

What about soil? Couldn't I just use regular garden soil, since that's what tomatoes usually grow in anyway?

Good potting soils do not occur naturally. They are manufactured. Even the best garden soil usually makes very poor soil for growing plants in containers. In the garden, soil has many tiny channels which allow water to pass from the surface down through the topsoil to the subsoil. Place that same soil in a pot and all the water applied to the surface must find its way out of one to four drainage holes. Drainage is greatly restricted.

Why wouldn't all this water in the soil be good for the plant?

The problem is that the water displaces air in between the soil particles. Air is just as essential to the functioning of roots as water.

Growing plants in containers is as old as Babylon, famous for its hanging gardens. But to be successful, certain basic techniques must be practised. In my opinion, tomato plants of an unknown variety growing in soil of unknown properties is not a good investment, even at sale prices.

Good potting soil is made up of coarse ingredients such as compost, fibrous sphagnum peat moss, perlite, vermiculite or coarse concrete-grade sharp sand, and the right type of garden soil. If, however, your garden soil sticks to your shoes right after a rain or resists cultivation when dry, it will likely cause trouble in a potting soil and should be left out.

If you have garden and kitchen residues that have been wel composted (Chapter 1), you may use up to one part in five and adjust the rest of the ingredients accordingly. A beginning mixtur can consist of one part good loamy garden soil, one part peat, one part either perlite or Numbers 2, 3 or 4 grade vermiculite or coarse washed concrete sand. Mix the ingredients thoroughly on the garage or basement floor and then do a drainage check. Loosely fill a 1 cm (6 in) pot with the mixture, and drop it on the floor from a heigh of about 15 cm (6 in) to settle it. Then flood the surface with wate Repeat the flooding as soon as the water has drained off the surface The second flood should disappear off the surface in sixty to ninet seconds. If it takes longer than this, then increase the amount c peat and perlite (or vermiculite or sand) and decrease the amoul of garden soil until the mixture meets the drainage requirement.

Rapid drainage indicates large porous spaces in the soil and a adequate air supply. As the water passes quickly through the sc and out the drainage holes, the whole soil is moistened but doe not remain saturated and air is pulled in through the surface t replace the drainage water— a healthy environment for roots. Mar packaged soils do not drain properly. If they do not meet the criteri then amend them with peat moss and perlite (or vermiculite or sand

While peat, perlite and vermiculite can be considered diseas and weed free, soil and sand cannot. The resultant mix can b sterilized by filling cake pans level full and placing them in a 105° (220°F) oven. Using a meat thermometer, raise the temperature the mix to 80°C (180°F) for thirty minutes. Over 100°C (212°F) an or longer than thirty minutes can cause chemical changes in the sc and kill beneficial soil bacteria. Under 71°C (160°F) and/or less tha twenty minutes will not kill some disease pathogens and weed seed

A simpler solution is to go to a reliable nursery and buy a prepare potting soil. However, I would check the drainage before you plar

Watering potted plants does require judgement. The most reliab test is to scratch down 10 to 20 per cent of the depth of the contain with a spoon or trowel. When it feels dry to the touch at this dep (use your knuckle, it's the most sensitive) the soil needs water. Cov the whole soil surface with a flood of water from a pitcher or pa A thin stream of water from a hose or watering can often finds way down through the soil without wetting much of the soil ba Water should be applied until 15 to 20 per cent runs out the drainag holes.

Drainage holes in the container are essential to prevent wat saturation. A large plastic saucer under the pot will collect drainag water. However, do not allow the root system of the plant to sit the drainage water for more than a few minutes. A simple wood block can be placed under the pot to hold it up out of the drainag water. A constantly available source of water at the base of a pot will move back up into the soil and displace the necessary air. A fertile, well-constructed and properly watered potting soil will be at least 20 per cent air by volume.

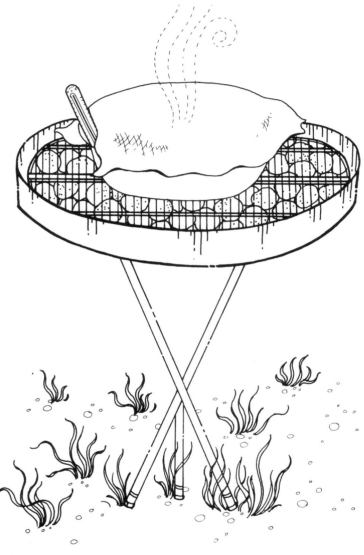

asteurizing compost

ou may run into objections to the smell when you sterilize potting soil in e oven indoors. It can be done nicely over an outdoor barbeque. A iece of canvas over the soil will speed up the process.

Growing Vegetables in Containers: Fertilizing

I am growing tomato plants in pots on my patio but they are producing only a fair crop. The upper foliage is green, but the lower leaves are all turning yellow. Can I stop this from happening?

What is the history of the soil used in the container?

I am not sure. I bought the plants already planted in the container at a sale.

How large is the container and the plant?

The plant is now about 1 m (39 in) high and the container is about 20 cm (8 in) high and wide.

Is the plant out where it's exposed to rain?

Yes, and I always water it thoroughly until water comes out the drainage holes.

I believe the basic problem with the yellow lower leaves and near normal coloured upper foliage is a lack of nitrogen fertilizer. Eventually most of the leaves will go pale green and then yellow. The growth rate will also drop off drastically. This nitrogen shortage is aggravated by a container that is too small for the type of plant you are attempting to grow. The minimum container size for a regular-sized tomato plant is 30 cm × 30 cm (12 in × 12 in), and 38 cm × 38 cm (15 × 15 in) would be even better. Your plants have nearly exhausted the nutrient supply and the upper leaves are now feeding on the plant food in the lower leaves. Also rain has a leaching effect on container soil, washing the nutrients out of the drainage holes. In a garden, the plant would send more roots out to pick up fertilizer elements. In a container, the only way the plant needs can be met is by repeated applications of fertilizer.

So I should fertilize, then.

Yes. I would drench the pots using a double-strength solution of 20-20-20 water-soluble fertilizer, the next three times when you would normally water. Then revert to normal strength every three weeks. You can be sure that if the nitrogen is low, then phosphorus and potash in 20-20-20 are also required.

Although good potting soil should have the correct fertilizer leve to begin root action, fertilizing with a water-soluble 20-20-20 or 1 28-14 analysis should begin within ten days after the plants a planted. With rapidly expanding plants like tomatoes, cucumbe and other vegetables growing in full sunlight, I recommend dilu fertilizing with every watering. Mix 5 mL of water-soluble fertilizer p 4.5 litres of water (1 level teaspoon per gallon).

Another simple way of obtaining the necessary plant nutrients is a single application of osmocote — a controlled-release water-soluble fertilizer (see p. 24). The retail containers of osmocote 14-14-14 prescribe the amount for each container size. Scatter this amount on the soil surface and water will carry the fertilizer from the capsules to the roots.

I would not use granular garden fertilizer on potted plants. It is not possible to mix enough of this type of fertilizer into the initial mixture to supply the plant's needs for the duration of the crop. If you did, you would burn the roots with the high fertilizer salts at the beginning. The only exception to this, if it is readily available to you, is superphosphate (0-20-0) and finely ground agricultural limestone (calcium carbonate). Both ingredients are slowly soluble and will eventually be required by the plants. Apply at the rate of 250 mL (1 cup) of each per wheelbarrow (3 cu ft) of mix.

Gardening in the Bag

I live in an apartment and would love to grow some cucumbers on my balcony.

What direction does the balcony face?

Mostly east. We get about half a day's sun.

You should be able to grow most vegetables in this situation. Full sun would be better but half a day is adequate.

Is there any way I can avoid having to cart up heavy bags of soil?

Yes, you can use peat-lite soilless mix. You can easily carry a 85 dm^3 (3 ft^3) bag under one arm.

What about containers?

If water draining from the container onto the balcony floor is no problem, you really do not need any container. You can use the peat-lite right in the bag. If you must collect the drainage water then you will have to use a conventional 30 to 35 cm (12 to 14 in) pot with a matching saucer. Any container you use should have drainage holes.

How do I grow plants in the bag?

Simply cut 2.5 cm (1 in) cross-shaped slits in one side of the bag; about two for every 20 dm^3 (1/2 bushel) of bag. Lay the bag down flat, holes down for drainage. Then plant your vegetables in slits cut in the top of the bag.

How many plants could I grow in one bag?

With tomatoes and cucumbers, you could grow about three or four. You should grow them vertically, confining the plant to one central stem by pruning off all suckers that form at each leaf node. The plants will require the support of a stout cord tied to the floor of the balcony above. Simply give the plants an occasional twist around the cord (see Chapter 2).

A simple, effective way of growing vegetables on a balcony, patio or even in a garden is to make use of the peat-lite soilless mix. It is lightweight, sterile, drains well and produces excellent crops. The bag can be the growing container. Once the drainage holes are made in the pillow-shaped bag, the holes in the upper surface are made to suit the plants grown. With plants like tomatoes and cucumbers, three or four cross-shaped slits 15 cm (6 in) long are spaced-out evenly on the surface. Insert a 15 cm (6 in) or larger funnel in each hole and keep filling it with water until the water stops draining out of the funnel. With the 85 dm³ (3 ft³) bag, you may need a couple of extra holes to get the whole bag moist. With other vegetables like lettuce or herbs, you can cut a window out of most of the surface of the bag and plant at the appropriate spacing (see Chapters 2 and 8). The minimum-sized bag I would use is 60 dm³ (2 ft³), which would support one tomato or cucumber plant.

About the only problem with planting in the bag is watering. The bigger bags 85 dm³ (3 ft³) will present less of a watering problem than smaller 20 dm³ (1/2 bushel) bags. A bag with four plants will need 4.5 to 9 L (1 to 2 gal) of water a day and may require watering twice a day when the plants are 2 m (6 ft) tall and loaded with fruit. When the tomatoes are first planted, the demand may only be .6 L (1 pt) per plant per day.

Dr. Raymond Sheldrake of Cornell University, originator of peat-lite mixes,suggests watering with the same funnel by re-inserting it into the bag and pouring the water in the middle of the bag or in two separate locations. The water should stop flowing from the funnel when the peat-lite is sufficiently moist.

Another Sheldrake suggestion is a 4.5 L (1 gal) plastic jug fitted with a plastic tubing 5 mm inside diameter. A water-tight joint can be made in the side of the jug close to the bottom by drilling a hole fractionally smaller than the tubing. The tubing is then pressed into the hole. This tubing is extensively used by greenhouses and nurseries and should be available from them. Automatic watering over your vacation can be achieved by using a large plastic pail rather than the jug. With the jug hung high and a screw clamp on the tubing, you could drip water over a long period. The constant liquid fertilizing program used by professional growers could be approximated by adding a low rate of liquid fertilizer to the water. Add

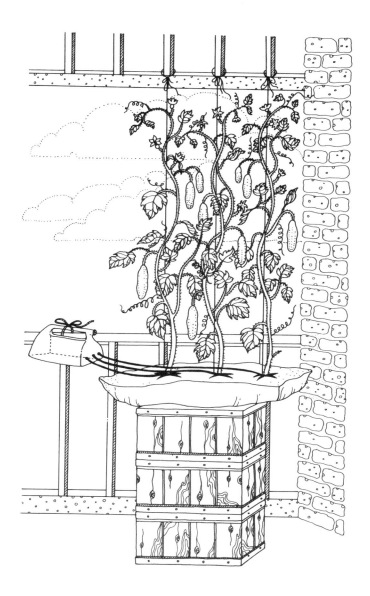

Gardening in the bag
Where an opaque wall is below the railing, raise the bag of peat-lite up on a small table or crates so that the plants receive sun. As the plants grow, they can be lowered closer to the ground.

about 7 mL (1/2 tblsp of 20-20-20 water-soluble fertilizer to 4.5 L (1 gal) of water and use this solution for watering. Drainage through the bottom of the bag is essential.

If a constant liquid fertilizing is not used, nutrients could be applied with each watering or once a week. If fertilizing only once a week, use about 14 to 28 mL (1 to 2 tblsp) of 20-20-20 water-soluble fertilizer per 4.5 L (1 gal).

For automatic watering you will need one plastic jug for each bag and 1 m (36 in) of tube per 20 dm^3 (1/2 bushel) of peat-lite. About 500 g of water-soluble 20-20-20 fertilizer will last a full season. With this modest investment, you should be able to produce 9 kg (20 lb) of tomatoes per plant — an excellent return.

With plants like tomatoes and cucumbers, make three or four cross-shaped slits spaced evenly on the surface of the bag. Watering can be done through a funnel.

Chapter 8: Herb Gardening

Kinds of Herbs

I'm really into gourmet cooking along with my gardening, and I have become interested in growing my own herbs. What conditions do they require?

Most herbs need at least six to eight hours of direct sunlight to produce the oils needed for fragrance and taste. Generally, they do not require soil high in plant nutrients (fertilizer). The fragrant and flavourful oil is produced most abundantly on less fertile soil. This does not mean they will thrive in subdivision subsoil. Once a site is chosen which gives adequate light, deep digging, preferably to 45 cm (18 in) is desirable. Incorporate an 8 cm (3 in) application of peat moss if the plot has not successfully grown vegetables before. Good drainage is essential, particularly for the perennial herbs.

Do they require regular watering like other vegetables?

Only to get them established, during the first month of growth. After this, most herbs perform best in a rather arid situation, receiving water only in times of deep drought.

Being a gourmet cook, our questioner undoubtedly knew the flavours she was after and the herbs she needed to grow to get them. Following is a list of herbs with pertinent information on propagation, culture, use and harvesting.

ANGELICA *Angelica archangelica:* Stems and flower petioles (they have a sweet celery scent) can be added to salads. They can also be blanched in boiling water and eaten like celery or cooked with rhubarb; also candied and used as a garnish for cakes, candy and desserts. Leaves are cooked with fish, slew and soups.
Angelica is a bold accent plant that will tolerate partial shade. They are biennial in nature, so some must be sown from fresh seed (they lose their viability quickly) in July or August each year, to flower the second year. Growth can attain 2 m (6 1/2 ft) so allow at least 61 cm × 61 cm (24 × 24 in) per clump. One of the few herbs that responds well to shade, rich soil and constant moisture.

ANISE *Pimpinella anisum:* The licorice-like flavour from its green leaves and seeds is used in salads, meats and baking. It is a slow-growing annual attaining a height of 46 cm (18 in) so plants should be spaced about 30 cm (12 in) apart in a row. Leaves are harvested fresh; seeds are allowed to mature, dried, removed from stems and stored. Seeds can be sown each year in the garden in late April or sown in March and grown as transplants indoors.

ANISE HYSSOP *Agastache foeniculum:* Both the flower and foliage are anise-scented. Fresh leaves are used as a garnish in cold drinks and fruit cups. Dried leaves can be used to make "tea" and in sachets and potpourri. The plant is a handsome, erect perennial, highly ornamental as a background plant in a perennial border. Both flowers and foliage are decorative in dried arrangements, retaining their colour and fragrance. Grown from seed sown in fall or spring, the 90 to 120 cm (3 to 4 ft) established plants also self-sow seeds which are readily transplanted. They also self-multiply by root division so allow 60 to 90 cm (24 to 36 in) per plant in a permanent location.

BORAGE *Borago officinalis:* Young fresh leaves have a cucumber-like taste which adds this subtle flavour to salads, soups, and stews. It can also be cooked as a vegetable. Flowers provide colour in potpourri and are candied for use in fruit drinks and cups.
   As an annual, borage is grown from seeds which germinate readily. Mature plants allowed to go to seed will self-sow, producing stronger plants than transplants. They require full sun and do best in light, sandy soil. Sow directly into the garden in early spring, allowing about 51 cm × 51 cm (20 in × 20 in) per plant. Attains a mature height of about 76 cm (30 in).

CARAWAY *Carum carvi:* A biennial, the familiar seeds are produced in the second year of growth and harvested in the autumn. The carrot-like leaves are used to flavour soups and salads. Seeds are used to flavour bread, cheese, sauerkraut, cakes, cookies and baked apples. Roots are also edible. About 76 cm (30 in) at maturity, the upright plants are produced from transplants or seeds sown in the spring or early fall, allowing about 46 cm × 46 cm (18 in × 18 in) per plant. Caraway plants like full sun but are tolerant of light shade. Light, dry soil is preferred.

CHERVIL *Anthriscus cerefolium:* Fresh or dried leaves are used as a garnish for fish, soups, omelettes or mixed with salad greens. Chervil is fennel-flavoured but more aromatic. The parsley-like, ferny leaves are best used fresh but preserve well by freezing. An annual plant, seeds are sown in fall and every three or four weeks beginning in early spring. Allow 15 cm by 38 cm (6 in by 15 in) per plant. This is one of the few herbs that responds to partial shade and fertile organic soil.

CHIVES *Allium schoenoprasum:* A hardy, readily expanding perennial plant growing to about 40 cm (15 in) from clusters of bulbs. The slender, onion-like foliage has a mild onion fragrance and flavour, and is used fresh to flavour meat, omelettes, salads, soups, vegetables, cheese and egg dishes, cottage cheese and sour cream. Bulbs can be pickled like small onions and used to flavour meat. Chives are propagated by dividing roots in either the spring or fall. Clumps ought to be divided every three years to maintain vigour. A small clump that can be encompassed by your thumb and forefinger is enough to establish a new plant. It will also self-sow prolifically unless the attractive purple flowers are kept from maturing. Chives prefer full sun and moderately rich and moist soil but will tolerate lesser conditions. Harvest them fresh, cutting the leaves at the bottom. Shearing the tops off results in an unnatural brush-cut appearance. Flavour is retained better by freezing than drying. It takes about a week to accomplish drying for storage.

CLARY SAGE *Salvia sclarea:* Leaves can be added to omelettes and sometimes used to flavour wine and beer. Leaves act as a fixative in potpourri and sachets. The 1 to 1 1/2 m (3 to 5 ft) plants are biennial, flowering the second year. Sow in the spring or early fall, allowing about 61 × 61 cm (24 in × 24 in) per plant when transplanted or thinned. Mature plants allowed to go to seed will self-sow, otherwise sowings each year are necessary. Clary sage requires full sun, average soil, and will likely rot in a poor drainage situation.

CORIANDER *Coriandrum sativum:* These erect, 60 cm (24 in) rather sparse-growing annual plants have a sweet, spicy scent at maturity. The ground fruit is used to flavour pastries, puddings, apple sauce, baked apples and pears, salads, hamburger and bread sausage. Fresh leaves can be used sparingly in salad, stew and Chinese and South American dishes. Coriander tastes and smells like orange leaves in stuffings and curries. It is best started in March from seed sown indoors or in a heated frame and transplanted to a full sun location allowing 30 × 60 cm (12 × 24 in) per plant. Sandy soil is ideal.

DILL *Anethum graveolens:* One of the most popular and easy-to-grow annual savoury herbs. Leaves are used fresh or dried to flavour pickles, fish, steaks, chops, poultry, lamb, omelettes, cottage cheese, soup, sauces, and potato salad. The seed is used in pickling cucumbers. Dill is readily grown from seed beginning in the early spring or fall, and is somewhat difficult to transplant because of its long taproot. Plants self-sow prolifically but are short lived and it is necessary to make successive sowings three weeks to a month apart. Sow in rows 30 cm (24 in) apart, thinning plants to about 10 cm

(4 in) apart. Does best in full sun and moderately fertile, well-drained soil. The plants grow 61 to 91 cm (2 to 3 ft). The leaves are most flavourful just as the flowers open and can be preserved by freezing. Harvest seeds by cutting the whole plant and hanging it in a breezy, protected place.

FENNEL *Foeniculum vulgare:* A branching 1 1/2 m (4 to 5 ft) perennial plant which requires 61 cm × 61 cm (24 in × 24 in) for each plant. Seeds are used to flavour salads, omelettes, sauerkraut, bread, pudding, and apple pie. Leaves are best used fresh in fish, soups, stews, salads, pork and veal. Fennel is usually grown from seed but the tap root makes transplanting difficult so sow it directly where you want it and then thin out. The plant prefers an alkaline soil, low fertility and full,hot sun.

FLORENCE *azoricum:* Another variety of fennel, this is a smaller annual with a thickened, bulb-like base. Flower stalks can be harvested just before bloom and eaten like celery.

GARLIC *Allium sativum:* Sets (cloves) are planted early each spring at 8 cm (3 in) intervals and covered with 1 cm (1/2 in) soil. By fall, the pungent cloves have multiplied and are dug up and dried. Garlic grows best in full sun in good garden soil and with an adequate supply of moisture. The flat, onion-like leaves reach about 61 cm (24 in) at maturity in late August. When leaves have lost their green colour and are bent over, the garlic is ready for harvest. Dig them up, remove leaves that come off readily and dry in a breezy covered place. Clean and store at room temperature in open jars. While garlic users could never pass a social breathalizer test, many love it with meats, in salad, vegetable sauces. Garlic salt is obtained from pulverised dry cloves.

LEMON BALM *Melissa officinalis:* The leaves of this self-branching bushy 1 m (39 in)perennial herb with its distinct lemon scent are used to flavour salads, soups, fish, stews, poultry, vegetables, fruit cups, cold drinks and egg dishes. Lemonbalm and its yellow variegated mutation, "Aurea," are grown from seeds that germinate slowly. Sow in fall or spring and allow about 30 by 90 cm (12 × 36 in) per plant in full light and average, well-drained soil. The plant may also be propagated by soil layering, root division and by rooting 10 cm (4 in) cuttings prior to flowering. Lemon balm forms broad clumps by spreading underground rhizomes. Leaves can be used fresh or dried and used later.

LEMON GERANIUM *Pelargonium crispum:* This is a pretty ornamental plant that also gives fragrance to sachets and potpourri. It can be propagated by rooting 8 cm (3 in) cuttings. Other members of the Pelargonium or geranium family are the scented geraniums such as rose, peppermint and apple. These can also be used in sachets and potpourri. The extracted oils give a sophisticated scent to soap and toiletries.

LEMON VERBENA *Lippia citriodora:* Propagated by rooting 8 cm (3 in) cuttings, this tender, shrubby perennial must be wintered indoors in Canada. It is grown for its fragrance and to give a lemony taste to beverages. The narrow, shiny leaves are stripped individually from the plant and dried on screens.

LOVAGE *Levisticum officinale:* The leaves of this 1.5 m (5 ft) perennial are used sparingly to flavour salads, soups, stews, vegetables, meat dishes, chicken and gravy. Stems and flower petioles can be candied or blanched and used as a vegetable. Seeds are used to flavour meat, candy and bread. Lovage can be grown from fresh seed sown in the fall or by root division in the spring. It also self-sows readily. Another herb that is the exception to the rule in that it will tolerate partial shade and prefers moist, well-drained, fertile soil. Leaves can be used fresh or dried on a screen.

MINT *Mentha spicata:* Spreading by surface and underground rhizomes, the aggressive-growing perennial mint can take over the garden unless systematically restrained by cultivation around the clump. Confinement, not propagation, is generally the problem once you obtain the first root division from a nursery in the spring. There are several variations in flavour. The most popular selections are spearmint *(Mentha spicata),* peppermint, *(Mentha peperita),* and lemon mint, *(Mentha citrata).* Maturing at about 61 cm (24 in) in height and requiring 61 cm × 61 cm (24 in × 24 in) per clump, mint can be harvested fresh from late spring through the summer, and it tends to thrive on heavy harvesting. Highly useful to flavour vinegar dressing used on lamb, jellies, sauces, fruit cups, ice drinks and vegetables as well as confections and mint tea. Leaves are picked individually from the plant just as flowering begins and are then air dried on screen. Mint will tolerate partial shade.

OREGANO *Origanum vulgare:* The pungent leaves can be used fresh or dry to flavour tomato dishes, meat, poultry and pork stuffing, vegetables and egg dishes. The 76 cm (2 1/2 ft) tall perennial plants can be propagated by seeds sown in early spring, by rooting early summer cuttings and by root division of existing clumps in the early spring. Established clumps self-sow prolifically. Allow about 51 cm × 51 cm (20 in × 20 in) per clump in full sun and average soil. Divide clumps every three years to maintain vigour. Oregano is harvested by cutting the stalks when plants start to flower. Hang them to dry for two weeks, remove the leaves, crumble and store in jars.

PARSLEY *Petroselinun crispum:* Leaves of this popular, easy to grow, savoury herb are used fresh and dried to flavour fish, soups, stews, sauces, vegetables, egg dishes and salads. Reported to be rich in vitamins C and A and iron. Actually a biennial, flowering the second year, parsley is usually grown as an annual (flavour is best the first year). It is propagated from seeds which are very hard and slow to germinate, taking as long as six weeks. Overnight soaking in warm water speeds up germination. Due to slow germination, seeds sown about 1 in apart directly into rows in the garden in April can be lost unless sown along with something like radish which come up quickly and act as an edible row marker. Five to ten seeds can also be sown directly into peat or plastic 7 cm (3 in) pots early in March and transplanted into the garden in late April. While parsley will tolerate partial shade, it does best in fertile, open soil and full sun, spacing plants about 15 cm (6 in) apart. There are several cultivars of the curly-leaf type offered in good seed catalogues plus a strong flavoured flat leaf type (Italian, *neopolitanum*) and parsnip rooted type (Hamburg, *tuberosum*). The curly-leaf type is considered less winter hardy than the flat-leaf. Both leaves and roots keep their flavour when dried or frozen.

ROSEMARY *Rosemarinus officinalis:* The spicy, pine-scented leaves are used fresh or dry to flavour lamb, pork, poultry, beef, stuffings, vegetables and salad dressing. Can be grown from seed sown indoors in late February or early March but seedlings are slow to develop. It is more readily propagated from stem cuttings, root division or soil layering in May or early June. Rosemary thrives in full sun, light, sandy alkaline soil or grown in 20 cm (8 in) containers. Rosemary is a perennial where ground does not freeze but must be wintered over indoors in harsher climates. The flavour of the leaves is at its peak when the flower is forming. Then they can be cut and dried (not in the oven, since oils are volatile). Rosemary does not freeze well.

SAGE *Salvia officinalis:* Leaves with their characteristic sharp, peppery scent are used in poultry and pork stuffing, sausages, cheese and egg dishes, cooked vegetables, fish and game. A shrubby perennial plant growing to about 76 cm (30 in), sage does best in full sun, moderately fertile soil that must be well drained to avoid winter kill. Sage will go scraggly without annual pruning down almost to the ground to promote bushy growth. Each clump will easily use up 61 cm × 61 cm (24 in × 24 in) of space. Leaves and the leafy top of stalks should be cut when flowers begin to form and then dried. Freezing is not recommended.

SUMMER SAVOURY *Satureja hortensis:* A spice-scented, bushy 46 cm (18 in) annual which will grow from seeds sown 6 mm

(1/4 in) deep directly into a garden row, ten to twelve seeds per 30 cm (12 in) and not thinned. Successive sowings three weeks apart are necessary to maintain a fresh supply. Summer savoury may have to be staked to prevent toppling of top-heavy plants. Leaves are used fresh or dried to flavour soups, egg dishes, sauces, stuffings, stews, fried potatoes, beans, peas and salad. Final harvest is when the plants are starting to flower by cutting stalks and hanging them to dry.

SWEET BASIL *Ocimum basilicum:* A tender, warmth-loving, frost-sensitive annual that can be best started indoors as a transplant, sown six weeks prior to the frost-free date in your area. Transplant plants about 30 cm (12 in) apart outdoors when danger of frost is past into a full sun, fertile location and supply even moisture. Pinching out tops just after transplanting encourages branching. Leaves are used fresh or dry to enhance tomato dishes, soups, stew, sauces, spaghetti, meat, game, fish, poultry and egg dishes. Leaves can be harvested for fresh use any time. For storage, cut stalks when the basil is starting to flower, hang and dry for two weeks. Can be frozen but drying preserves the flavour better.

SWEET CICELY *Myrrhis ordorata:* The fleshy roots of this 1 m (39 in) perennial can be boiled and eaten as a vegetable or used in a salad. Leaves, dried or fresh, can be used to flavour soups, stews and seafood. The slow-growing, erect plants take several years to reach a mature size so plant them in a location where they remain undisturbed. Propagated from seeds sown in the fall, as freezing and thawing aids germination. Mature plants tend to self-sow. Cicely can also be propagated by root division in the fall. A partially shaded, moist location is best but the soil must be well drained. The whole plant is anise-scented.

SWEET MARJORAM *Majorana hortensis:* The leaves are used fresh or dried to flavour a wide variety of meat dishes. This is a tender perennial best treated as an annual in most parts of the country or brought indoors in winter as a pot plant. It can be propagated by crown division of an existing clump (see page 143), cuttings taken in May or June or seeds sown indoors six to eight weeks ahead of the frost-free date in your area. Transplant these into bedding plant containers and outdoors in May about 20 cm (8 in) apart. Full sun and average soil fertility are fine. Stalks are cut when they start to flower and hung to dry.

TARRAGON, "FRENCH" *Artemesia dranunculus:* The plant is propagated only by spring division of root crowns as French tarragon does not produce seeds. A hardy perennial, the roots need a frozen dormancy period each year to sustain vigorous growth. French tarragon can also be propagated by rooting 8 cm (3 in) cuttings in late May or June. It prefers full sun and well-drained, sandy soil or highly organic clay loam. It will, however, tolerate a poor, dry soil but will rot in a badly drained location. Fresh or dried leaves are frequently called for in recipes to flavour steaks, chops, seafood, chicken, egg dishes and a variety of sauces and salad dressings. This herb is best used fresh as some flavour is lost in drying.

THYME *Thymus vulgaris:* An unstable species that has many variants. The 20 to 30 cm (8 to 12 in) bushy, perennial plants are evergreen but may need a winter mulch of straw or evergreen boughs. Leaves or flowering tops are used alone or in combination with other herbs to flavour meat, fish, poultry, game, chowders, stews, stuffings, vegetables, cheese and egg dishes. Propagated by 8 cm (3 in) stem cuttings in May or June, by spring root division or seed sown in early March as an indoor transplant. Often they are grown as an ornamental border or rockery plant where it spreads prolifically, making a fragrant ground cover. The leafy tops and flower clusters are cut and hung to dry for winter use.

Bringing a Herb Garden Indoors

I brought my rosemary plant indoors. It was watered and in good light but by the end of November it had dried up completely. I don't seem to have any luck with parsley or thyme, either.

Do you grow the rosemary in the garden and then pot it up in the fall?

Yes, but it did get a reasonable amount of soil with it.

As much as two thirds of the root system of the original plant would likely be lost in this digging operation, severely shocking the plant. The soil that you were able to keep with the remaining root system, being garden soil, would not really drain well enough to make a suitable potting soil. If you eventually intend to bring some of your herbs indoors for the winter, then I would grow them in good potting soil in a pot plunged into a sunny spot in the garden. Turn the pot once a month to prune the roots going out the drainage holes. This will prevent future shock.

Would this make my herbs dry up and die?

It would certainly be a contributing factor. The other factors are the high indoor temperature relative to the amount of light available. Herbs grow well outdoors at room temperature and above but the light is correspondingly greater. To compensate for the much lower light in your home in the fall and winter, it would be a great advantage to have the pots in your brightest window with a room

138

temperature between 8° to 14°C (46° to 57°F). However, probably the most significant factor causing deterioration of rosemary indoors is low humidity. Misting the plant with a fine spray two or three times a day is often recommended, but this does little good because it changes the humidity for such a brief period. A mechanical humidifier will bless your plants and you and it is part of the best solution. Grouping plants together allows the plants' natural transpiration to raise the humidity. Sitting the plants in a large plastic saucer which is kept full of water with the pot raised so that the plant's root system does not contact the water also helps raise humidity.

What about debugging it? I know there are some fungus gnats about.

Two applications of diazinon (5 per cent) granules on the soil and watered in two weeks apart will control the larvae of fungus gnats. The gnat itself must be controlled at the same time by spraying with an aerosol spray containing the active ingredient of resmethrin.

Our palates are becoming increasingly sophisticated and nowhere is this more evident than in the use of herbs. It's only natural to want to extend the availability of fresh herbs into the fall and winter. Many, of course, have too large a growth habit and root system but some are quite suitable. These can include any of the mints which are propagated by root division or by taking 8 cm (3 in) cuttings from the growing tip of the plant. One selection of the mint family, Corsican mint *(Mentha requienii)* is particularly suitable. Its attractive, trailing growth is suitable for a hanging basket. Both regular and dwarf basil can be readily grown indoors from seed. Chives can be root divided from an existing clump in the spring and potted for indoor use later. Parsley can be grown from seed from a spring sowing and transplanted into as deep a pot as possible. It has a deep tap root you must accommodate. A new dwarf strain of curly parsley, called Curlina, is ideal for pot culture. Slow growing thyme is useful and can be root divided and potted from an existing clump or obtained from an early spring sowing of seed or by rooting 8 cm (3 in) cuttings. Sweet marjoram can also be grown from seed.

Most garden centres now stock these and other herbs especially in the spring. Repot these into a 10 to 15 cm (4 to 6 in) pot using a good potting soil and then plunge the pots into a sunny spot in the garden to be brought indoors in the fall for winter use.

Should insects prove to be a problem, and they seldom are on savoury herbs, rotenone and sevin dust are effective and safe to use on edible crops.

Harvesting and Drying Herbs

What is the best way to dry herbs? Would it be fastest just to pick them and let them dry in the sun?

I would not recommend sun drying because it destroys the fragrant, flavourful oils. For long-stemmed herbs, cut as indicated in the descriptions given earlier in the chapter, wash the base of the stem of any soil and remove the dead leaves. Bundle, tie and label each kind and hang the bundles in a breezy location out of the rain.

What is the best time to harvest?

A dry, sunny morning after the dew has disappeared and before the hot sun has dissipated the oils is the best time to harvest.

Next to the flavour they impart to your food, one of the great joys of growing herbs is the fragrant harvest. The descriptions given earlier indicate those that can be harvested fresh. The only limitation here is not to harvest so severely that growth is arrested. The leaves are the factory that bring about growth and some must always be left to do the job.

For short-stemmed herbs and seeds, drying screens work well. An old window fly screen or one simply constructed of 3 by 5 cm (1 by 2 in) lumber would do nicely. This allows air circulation from all sides. If a thin layer is placed on the screen, the drying of leaves usually takes about a week with screens placed in a breezy location protected from rain and sun. Seeds take longer. After the initial weeks of drying, rub the seeds and hulls and gently blow away the hulls. Try a hairdryer set on low for this threshing operation.

Once the herbs have been stored in air-tight jars, you would be wise to check each one for signs of moisture. This will cause rapid deterioration. If moisture is detected, the herbs should go through the drying process again.

Propagating Herbs from Cuttings

My neighbour has some tall oregano plants and she says I can take a few cuttings to plant in my garden. When is the best time to do this?

This can be done any time in the spring or early summer, taking 7 to 10 cm (3 to 5 in) cuttings from the tip of a healthy, vigorously growing plant. They should snap off but a knife might be necessary on some species. Keep leaves moist, out of the sun and in plastic bags or moist cloth if they have to be held for anything more than a few minutes.

Can I just plant them in any sized pot or container?

140

Any sterile container with drainage will do for rooting. However, a plastic bedded plant flat will not drain as well as a 10 cm (4 in) full-depth pot, due to the shallow depth of the soil.

A simple, sterile and effective rooting media is half peat moss and half vermiculite or perlite thoroughly mixed and moistened. About 2 cm (3/4 in) of the stem is tucked into the rooting media. If the leaves are closely spaced on the stem, they do not want to be buried and may have to be removed from the bottom 2 cm (3/4 in) of the stem. Space the cuttings so that the leaves are just touching. Moisten the media and leaves and put one or more pots in a clear plastic bag that does not flop down around the plants. Cuttings must not be allowed to wilt, so further misting may be necessary. Place the pots in bright diffused light at room temperature. The plastic bag may be closed at the initial stages of rooting and opened for progressively longer periods as the plants begin to root.

Rooting should take three to six weeks and can be detected by gently tugging on the cutting. The first resistance to the upward pull indicates the formation of root initials, firm resistance means the plastic should be completely removed. Acclimatize the plants by putting them in full sun and wind for longer periods until they are tough enough to be moved to their permanent location outdoors.

Sowing Herbs Outdoors

I want to start a herb garden outdoors. Is there anything special I need to do to get the garden ready to sow seeds in?

For those herbs that propagate by sowing seeds in a nursery bed and then transplanting, I would choose a sheltered spot that has open soil that can be readily kept moist. Hard soil that bakes in the heat is not suitable but for seedlings a great depth of suitable soil is not needed either. The top 5 cm (2 in) can be amended to contain 40 per cent peat, 40 per cent sharp sand and 20 per cent native soil. Then level with fine rake. I suggest you sow in short rows, clearly identified. Fine seed can be sown more readily if it is mixed with corn meal. Take time spacing the seeds, trying to achieve about 1 cm (1/2 in) between them. Carefully cover the seeds to a depth of not more than twice the thickness of the seed. Water with a fine nozzle and keep the soil moist.

Won't it be difficult to keep the soil moist in midsummer?

Yes, but you can use one thickness of burlap over the area until the seeds begin to sprout. Moisten the soil, apply the burlap, then thoroughly moisten it. The burlap must be removed as the seeds germinate to avoid seedling stretch from low light. After germination thin out the rows to about a 3 cm (1 in) spacing between seedlings as soon as the weakest seedlings can be pulled out. Remember, you will likely need a small number of plants, often just one or two. Transplanting into the final location is best done on a rainy or cloudy day or late in the day. Try to take a small clump of soil with the roots of each seedling and transplant at same depth as in the nursery bed. Be prepared to nurse the transplants with frequent light waterings until they root out into their new environment.

Where fall seeding is recommended, sow just before the ground freezes to prevent premature germination and winter kill of the seedlings. The instructions on sowing, growing and transplanting vegetable plants indoors (Chapter 7) apply also to herbs.

Soil Layering Herbs

I read instructions on propagating some herbs that call for soil layering. How is that done? Is it a good method?

Propagation by soil layering does remove some of the risk from the rooting process because the cutting remains on the parent plant

Soil layering
Anchor the stem down with a hairpin or staple and support the vertical tip with a small stake.

while rooting is accomplished. This ensures a supply of moisture and nutrients. Select a vigorous, near-horizontal stem or one flexible enough to bend and touch the ground. Starting at a point 15 cm (6 in) from the tip of this stem clear off all leaves for a space of about 15 cm (6 in). Loosen the soil where this cleared portion of the stem touches down. If the soil is not open and friable, then add up to 50 per cent by volume of peat moss. Excavate a narrow furrow in this cultivated soil that will allow the plucked portion of the stem to be buried to a depth of 5 cm (2 in). At the same time bend the end of the stem vertical.

Won't the bending break the stem?

The bending is usually only sufficient to put cracks in the outside of the cleared stem which promotes callusing and root initials. However, if this does not happen then gently scrape the bark off the buried portion of the stem. Pin the stem down with a hairpin or large staple and support the vertical tip with a small stake. Rooting should be accomplished in three to six weeks. Then the new plant can be pruned off the parent and planted in its permanent location.

Soil layering can be done any time from early summer until fall. The new plant can even be left on the parent plant over winter to be moved to its new home in the spring.

Multiplying Herbs by Division

I have some oregano that is supposed to be divided periodically. Do I just pull it apart until I have a single piece with some roots?

This is not usually a good idea. Most of the root system is lost and the new plant takes a long time to recover. Dig out the old clump intact if possible. The objective is to separate off a small clump — somewhat less than a handful. If this cannot be readily pulled off the parent clump with the roots intact, then cut it off with a large knife. Less damage to the roots will be done this way.

The description of each species given earlier indicates whether periodic division of perennial herbs is of benefit. Early spring is probably the best time to do this, allowing the new plants to become established before the stressful summer weather. Usually less damage is done if the whole parent plant is dug up and the crown cut vertically into small 5 to 10 cm (2 to 4 in) sections. Replant at the correct spacing (see individual herbs) and be prepared to water if rain does not occur at the right time.

Freezing Herbs

Can herbs be frozen for future use? I'm overrun with chives now but I know I'll want them in the winter.

Many herbs freeze very well, maintaining their summer flavour. Harvest the herb during the peak flavour period (see earlier descriptions of individual herbs for information on the best harvesting time). A food processor with a knife attachment is a fast way of reducing bulk. Process until finely chopped. You will need to have some idea of the amount you will use in your favourite recipes and have small plastic bags on hand to store that amount.

What if the recipe only calls for a spoonful or two?

Freeze thin layers in sandwich bags which can be opened. The required amount can then be broken off and the rest returned to the freezer. Remember to mark the contents of the bags clearly with a felt pen. Frozen herbs are not readily identified.

Seeds and plants of a wide variety of herbs and unusual plants are available from:
Otto Richter & Son Ltd., Goodwood, Ontario, L0C 1A0
Ashby's Seeds, R.R. #2, Cameron, Ontario, K0M 1G0

Government Bulletins

There is a wealth of sound information available on a wide range of vegetable and fruit gardening subjects. Most bulletins are written specifically for the home gardener in clear, concise language. The following list includes publications by federal and provincial agricultural departments plus the United States Department of Agriculture and the agricultural departments of the northeastern states.

How to Use This List

If you live in the Atlantic provinces and want the best strawberry varieties for that region, check the list under "s" for strawberries. You will find the listings "A.P. 232-641 STRAWBERRIES, Recommended Varieties" and "A.P. Nova Scotia Certified STRAWBERRY Nurseries."

Where to Send for Bulletins

Addresses of the various jurisdictions publishing bulletins are given at the end of the alphabetical listing. Federally published bulletins are available to all citizens of both countries. Provincial and state bulletins are available to citizens of that province or state. Most jurisdictions, however, will send a limited number of bulletins out of the country, province or state. If the state has a published policy on non-resident orders, this is shown following the address of the order office of that state.

Cost of Bulletins

Where no price is listed after the title of the bulletin, it is free. Where there is a charge, it is given after the title.

A.C.	Control of ANTS
A.C.	1298 Control of ANTS
U.S.D.A.	F2148 APHIDS on Leafy Vegetables
N.Y.	APHID
R.I.	APHIDS Pest Fact Sheet
A.C.	1431 Hybrid Seedling Rootstocks for APPLES
A.P.	C-6 Home Garden Production of APPLES
A.P.	The APPLE Maggot
B.C.	Growing APPLES
B.C.	Training APPLES
B.C.	Establishing APPLE Trees
B.C.	APPLE Varieties and Rootstocks
Ont.	74-092 APPLE Rootstocks
Conn.	78-18 Spray Guide for Home APPLE Orchards
Conn.	69-3 The APPLE MAGGOT and its Control
Conn.	Size Controlling APPLE Rootstocks
Conn.	75-68 Home Grown Fruit — APPLES
Mass.	L168 Varieties of APPLES for Massachusetts
Mass.	C102 Establishment and Managing of Compact APPLE Trees (75¢)
Mich.	E939 APPLE MAGGOT Control in Backyard Situations (15¢)

N.Y.	APPLE MAGGOTS
N.Y.	APPLE SCAB
N.Y.	APPLE Varieties in N.Y.S. (50¢)
R.I.	B201 APPLE Trees for the Homeowner
B.C.	APRICOTS Fact Sheet
Ont.	78-050 Growing APRICOTS
U.S.D.A.	G204 Growing APRICOTS for Home Use
Mich.	E533 APRICOTS Growing in Michigan (40¢)
N.Y.	Growing APRICOTS
A.P.	V1-75 ASPARAGUS
Alta.	FS254/20-1 ASPARAGUS for the Home and Market Garden
Conn.	67-66 Growing ASPARAGUS in the Home Garden
Mich.	E824(14) Family Vegetable Garden: ASPARAGUS and Rhubarb (5¢)
Mich.	E959 Know Your ASPARAGUS Pests (50¢)
R.I.	ASPARAGUS BEETLES
A.P.	V2-77 BEANS
Mich.	E966 Snap BEAN Insect Pests (10¢)
Mich.	E824(6) Family Vegetable Garden: Garden BEANS (5¢)
R.I.	NE-47 BEANS in the Home Garden
A.P.	V3-75 BEETS
U.S.D.A.	L360 Growing Table BEETS
B.C.	Production Guide for BERRY Crops
B.C.	BLACKBERRY Culture in British Columbia Plus Supplement
Ont.	78-032 Raspberries and BLACKBERRIES for the Home Garden
U.S.D.A.	G207 Thornless BLACKBERRIES for the Home Garden
Mass.	C115 Varieties of Raspberries and BLACKBERRIES in Massachusetts
N.Y.	BLACKBERRIES, Currants and Gooseberries (30¢)
A.C.	1279 High Bush BLUEBERRY Culture in Eastern Canada
A.C.	N36 Establishing Superior Low Bush BLUEBERRY Fields
A.P.	Hints on High Bush BLUEBERRY Growing in Nova Scotia
A.P.	Important Insects and Diseases on High Bush BLUEBERRY and Their Control
A.C.	837 Late BLIGHT of Potatoes and Its Control
B.C.	High Bush BLUEBERRIES Fact Sheet
Ont.	78-030 BLUEBERRIES in Ontario
Conn.	N3 High Bush BLUEBERRY Culture
Mass.	C173 Varieties of BLUEBERRIES for Massachusetts
Mich.	E564 Hints on Growing BLUEBERRIES (5¢)
N.Y.	BLUEBERRY Growing in the Home Garden
N.Y.	BLUEBERRY Insect and Disease Guide
R.I.	B143 High Bush BLUEBERRIES
U.S.D.A.	F2239 Growing Cauliflower and BROCCOLI
A.P.	210/24 BUDDING and Grafting for the Home Garden
Mass.	C116 Topworking and BUDDING of Fruit Trees
Mich.	E508 BUDDING and Grafting Fruit Trees (15¢)

A.P.	DAMPING OFF
A.C.	915 DISEASES, Insects and Mites on Stone Fruits
A.C.	1359 DISEASES and Pests of Potatoes
A.C.	1615 DISEASES of Carrots in Canada
A.P.	Important Insects and DISEASES on High Bush Blueberry and Their Control
A.P.	Strawberry DISEASES
A.P.	250/231 DISEASE Resistant Vegetable Varieties
A.P.	HG2-77 DISEASE and Insect Control in the Home Garden
B.C.	Peach Leaf Curl DISEASE
Ont.	64 Insect and DISEASE Control in the Home Garden
U.S.D.A.	AH376 Market DISEASES of Apples, Pears, and Quinces
U.S.D.A.	AH414 Market DISEASES of Stone Fruits: Cherries, Peaches, Apricots and Plums
U.S.D.A.	AH28 Market DISEASES of Tomato, Peppers and Eggplants
Conn.	NE31 Identifying DISEASES of Beans, Crucifers, Cucurbits, Peas, Sweet Corn, and Tomatoes (50¢)
Conn.	70-25 Currants and Gooseberries Insect and DISEASE Control
Conn.	75-25 Home Vegetable Garden DISEASE Control
Conn.	77-52 DISEASE Control for Potatoes in the Home Garden
Mich.	NCR45 DISEASES of Tree Fruits (75¢)
N.Y.	Insects and DISEASES of Vegetables in the Home Garden ($1.20)
N.Y.	DISEASE and Insect Control in the Home Orchard (25¢)
N.Y.	DISEASES of Tree Fruits ($1.35)
N.Y.	Insect and DISEASES of Stone Fruits
Pa.	S218 Plant DISEASES in Home Gardens (10¢)
Ont.	71-069 European EARWIG
Conn.	75-180 European EARWIGS
R.I.	EARWIG Pest Fact Sheet
Mich.	E971 Tomato, Pepper and EGGPLANT Insect Pests (10¢)
Mich.	E824(20) Family Vegetable Garden: EGGPLANTS (5¢)
A.C.	1280 ELDERBERRY Culture in Eastern Canada
Ont.	77-004 ELDERBERRIES
N.Y.	Growing ELDERBERRIES
Man.	FERTILIZER Recommendations for the Home Garden
U.S.D.A.	G89 Selecting FERTILIZERS for Lawn and Garden
Conn.	64-20 The Home Landscape Soils and FERTILIZERS
Conn.	75-13 Tree FERTILIZATION
Conn.	67-102 Lime, FERTILIZERS, and Manure for the Home Garden
Conn.	72-33 FERTILIZING Fruit Plantings
Mass.	L165 FERTILIZING Home Fruits
Mass.	C138 Natural FERTILIZERS in the Home Garden
Mich.	E852 FERTILIZERS for Fruit Trees (5¢)
N.Y.	FERTILIZING the Home Vegetable and Flower Garden
B.C.	FIREBLIGHT of Pear and Its Control
Ont.	FIREBLIGHT in Apple and Pear

148

A.C.	1370 Control of Rats and MICE
A.C.	1328 Control of MILLIPEDES
Conn.	72-45 MILLIPEDES
R.I.	Sowbugs, Pillbugs, and MILLIPEDES Pest Fact Sheet
U.S.D.A.	AB212 MINT Farming
A.C.	1592 Control of MOLES
B.C.	MOLE Control in British Columbia
Ont.	78-008 Polyethylene MULCHES in Vegetable Production
N.Y.	Seaweed as a Garden MULCH
N.Y.	Plastic MULCHES
Ohio	526 MULCHES for Home Grounds
A.P.	HG3-79 Growing MUSHROOMS at Home
U.S.D.A.	L509 MUSKMELON for the Home Garden
U.S.D.A.	AB379 Growing NECTARINES
Conn.	NE52 Home Orchard Peach and NECTARINE Culture
Penna.	NE52 Home Orchard Peach and NECTARINE Culture (10¢)
R.I.	NE52 Home Orchard Peach and NECTARINE Culture
R.I.	NURSERIES Offering Fruit Plants for Sale
Mass.	#41 NUTRICULTURE: A Guide to Soilless Culture of Plants
Conn.	AIB408 Growing Fruits and NUTS ($1.00)
Mich.	E824(23) Family Vegetable Garden: Lima Beans and OKRA (5¢)
A.P.	V10-78 ONIONS
Ont.	77-005 Artificial Curing of ONIONS
Ont.	75-066 ONION Drying
Ont.	76-019 ONION Neck Rot
Mich.	F972 Lettuce and ONION Insect Pests (10¢)
Mich.	E824(17) Family Vegetable Garden: ONIONS (5¢)
R.I.	ONION Maggot Pest Fact Sheet
A.P.	V24-75 ORGANIC Gardening
Mich.	E824(25) Family Vegetable Garden: ORGANIC Gardening
N.Y.	Facts about ORGANIC Gardening (25¢)
N.Y.	Companion Plants (ORGANIC Gardening)
N.Y.	Growing Vegetables ORGANICALLY (20¢)
R.I.	C173 ORGANIC Gardener's Guide to Pest Control
A.P.	V4-78 Carrots and PARSNIPS
A.P.	C13 Home Garden Production of PEACHES
B.C.	PEACHES Fact Sheet
B.C.	PEACH Leaf Curl Disease
U.S.D.A.	AN463 PEACH Production
Conn.	78-20 Spray Guide for Home PEACH Orchards
Conn.	NE52 Home Orchard PEACH and Nectarine Culture
Mass.	C117 Varieties of PEACHES for Massachusetts
N.Y.	PEACH Growing in N.Y.S. (50¢)
N.Y.	PEACH Tree Borers
N.Y.	PEACH Leaf Curl
Pa.	NE52 Home Orchard PEACH and Nectarine Culture (10¢)
R.I.	NE52 Home Orchard PEACH and Nectarine Culture

A.P.	C-7 Home Garden Production of PEARS
B.C.	PEARS Fact Sheet
U.S.D.A.	AH526 PEAR Production
Conn.	78-21 Spray Guide for Home PEAR Orchards
Mass.	L167 Varieties of PEARS and Quinces for Massachusetts
N.Y.	PEAR Culture (60¢)
A.P.	V12-77 PEAS
Mich.	E824(16) Family Vegetable Garden: PEAS (5¢)
N.Y.	Cornell PEAT-LITE Mix
A.P.	V13-77 PEPPER
Ont.	78-061 Growing PEPPERS
Mich.	971 Tomato, PEPPER and Eggplant Insect Pests (10¢)
Mich.	E824(20) Family Vegetable Garden: PEPPERS and Eggplants (5¢)
A.C.	1408 Gardening on PERMAFROST
B.C.	PEST Control for the Home Garden
Conn.	78-36 Synopsis of PESTICIDE Safety
N.Y.	Safe Use of PESTICIDES
Pa.	L336 Safe Use of PESTICIDES in the Home Garden (10¢)
Mass.	C121 Home Fruit PEST Control
Mich.	E751 PESTICIDE Manual (35¢)
Mich.	E824(13) Family Vegetable Garden: Controlling PESTS (5¢)
N.Y.	A Guide to Safe PEST Control
N.Y.	Handbook on Biological Control of Plant PESTS ($1.75)
A.C.	1359 Diseases and PESTS of Potatoes
Alta.	FS625 Control of Garden PESTS
R.I.	C73 Home Fruit PEST Control Guide
R.I.	C88 Home Vegetable PEST Cntrol Guide
R.I.	C173 Organic Gardener's Guide to PEST Control
R.I.	Sowbugs, PILLBUGS, and Millipedes Pest Fact Sheet
Mich.	E824(15) Starting PLANTS at Home (5¢)
A.P.	216/33 PLUM Varieties and Recommendations for the Annapolis Valley
A.P.	C12 Home Garden Production of PLUMS
B.C.	PLUMS and Prunes Fact Sheet
Conn.	78-22 Spray Guide for Home PLUM Orchard
Mass.	C170 Varieties of PLUMS for Massachusetts
N.Y.	Black Knot on PLUM and Cherry
B.C.	POLLINATION and Fruit Set in Tree Fruits
Ont.	76-013 Compatibility and POLLINATION of Fruit Varieties
Ont.	72-047 POLLINATION for Fruit and Seed Production
N.Y.	POLLINATION and Fruit Development
A.C.	1559 Growing Garden POTATOES
A.C.	1359 Diseases and Pests of POTATOES
A.C.	837 Late Blight of POTATOES and Its Control
A.C.	1530 Common Powdery Scab of POTATOES
Alta.	FS258/20-4 POTATOES for Home Gardeners
Alta.	FS258/625-1 Insect Control on POTATOES
A.P.	Atlantic Canada POTATO Guide
A.P.	257/630 POTATO Late Blight in the Home Garden
Man.	Growing POTATOES in the Home Garden

Ont.	78-085 POTATO Varieties
U.S.D.A.	AH474 POTATO Diseases
Conn.	77-52 Disease Control for POTATOES in the Home Garden
Conn.	78-34 Growing POTATOES in the Home Garden
Mich.	E570, E572, E573, E574, E575, E576 Bulletins on Various Disease Problems of POTATOES (5¢ ea.)
Mich.	E824(23) Family Vegetable Garden: POTATOES and Sweet Potatoes (5¢)
N.Y.	POTATOES in the Home Garden
N.Y.	Colorado POTATO Beetle
N.Y.	A Handbook on PROPAGATION ($1.75)
A.C.	1505 The PRUNING Manual
A.C.	1513 The PRUNING and Training of Fruit Trees
Ont.	77-006 Rules for PRUNING Fruit Trees
Ont.	73-097 PRUNING Oversize Spy Apple Trees
Conn.	74-27 PRUNING and Training Grapes
Conn.	PRUNING and Training Fruit Trees
Mass.	C108 PRUNING Fruit Trees in the Home Orchard
Mich.	E850 PRUNING Young Fruit Trees (10¢)
Ohio	528 PRUNING and Training Fruit Trees (45¢)
Pa.	S126 PRUNING for Fruit (30¢)
A.P.	V15-75 PUMPKINS and Squash
Mich.	E969 Cucumber, Melon, Squash, and PUMPKIN Insect Pests (10¢)
Mich.	E824(9) Family Vegetable Garden: Squash, PUMPKINS, Melons (5¢)
Mass.	C167 Varieties of Pears and QUINCES for Massachusetts
A.C.	1604 Control of RACCOONS
A.P.	V16-75 RADISH
A.C.	1447 Red RASPBERRY Cultivars for Eastern Canada
A.C.	1196 Growing Red RASPBERRIES in Eastern Canada
Alta.	FS230/20-1 RASPBERRIES in Alberta
A:P.	RASPBERRIES Variety Recommendations
A.P.	RASPBERRY, Home Garden Cultural Guide
B.C.	RASPBERRIES, Fact Sheet
Ont.	78-032 RASPBERRIES and Blackberries for the Home Garden
Conn.	NE45 Red RASPBERRY Culture
Mass.	C115 Varieties of RASPBERRIES and Blackberries for Massachusetts
Mich.	E542 Growing RASPBERRIES in Michigan (10¢)
N.Y.	Growing RASPBERRIES in the Home Garden
N.Y.	Virus Diseases of RASPBERRIES
N.Y.	RASPBERRY Growing in N.Y.S. (25¢)
N.Y.	RASPBERRY Cane Borer
R.I.	B203 RASPBERRY Culture
A.C.	1370 Control of RATS and Mice
A.C.	1369 RHUBARB Planting and Growing
A.P.	V17-75 RHUBARB

Ont.	76-044 RHUBARB Growing
U.S.D.A.	L555 RHUBARB Production
Mich.	E824(14) Family Vegetable Garden: Asparagus and RHUBARB (5¢)
Mich.	E851 ROOTSTOCKS for Fruit Trees (5¢)
A.C.	1075 Control of Root Maggots in RUTABAGAS
A.C.	1246 The SASKATOON
Ont.	74-113 SAPBEETLES
N.Y.	How to Save Vegetable SEED
N.Y.	Sowing SEEDS Indoors
A.C.	1605 Control of SKUNKS
A.C.	1213 Control of SLUGS
Ont.	77-008 SLUGS
N.Y.	SLUGS and Snails
R.I.	SLUGS Pest Fact Sheet
Conn.	64-20 The Home Landscape SOILS and Fertilizers
Mass.	#406 Do You Want to Make a Good SOIL Sample?
Pa.	C560 Garden SOIL and Its Care (10¢)
A.C.	1330 Control of SOWBUGS and Pillbugs
Conn.	72-41 SOWBUGS
R.I.	SOWBUGS Pest Fact Sheet
A.P.	V18-75 SPINACH
N.Y.	SPINACH Leaf Miner
R.I.	SPINACH LEAF MINER Pest Fact Sheet
N.Y.	Vegetable Garden SPRAY Guide
N.Y.	SPRAYING the Home Orchard
A.P.	V15-75 Pumpkins and SQUASH
B.C.	SQUASH, Vegetable Marrow and Pumpkin Fact Sheet
Conn.	NE51 Growing SQUASHES
Mich.	E969 Cucumber, Melon, SQUASH, and Pumpkin Insect Pests (10¢)
Mich.	E824(9) Family Vegetable Garden: SQUASH, Pumpkins and Melons (5¢)
N.Y.	SQUASH Vine Borer
R.I.	SQUASH BUGS Pest Fact Sheet
R.I.	SQUASH VINE BORER Pest Fact Sheet
R.I.	NE51 Growing SQUASHES
Mass.	NRAES-7 Home STORAGE of Fruits and Vegetables ($1.25)
Mich.	HG119 STORING Fruits and Vegetables (15¢)
Mich.	E824(11) Family Vegetable Garden: Drying and STORING (5¢)
N.Y.	Fruit and Vegetable STORAGE Room Plan (50¢)
N.Y.	Vegetable Harvest and STORAGE
N.Y.	STORING Vegetables and Fruits in Basements, Cellars (40¢)
A.C.	1585 STRAWBERRY Culture in Eastern Canada
Alta.	FS232/20 STRAWBERRIES in Alberta
A.P.	232-641 STRAWBERRIES Recommended Varieties
A.P.	624 Field Key to Insects and Other Pests Injuring the STRAWBERRY
A.P.	STRAWBERRY Diseases

Abbreviations and Addresses of Sources of Government Bulletins

A.C.:
Agriculture Canada
Information Services
Ottawa K1A 0C7

Alta, Alberta:
Publications Office
Alberta Agriculture
9718-107th St.
Edmonton, Alta. T5K 2C8

A.P. (Atlantic Provinces)
The Atlantic provinces cooperate in the production of agriculture bulletins under the umbrella of the Atlantic Horticultural Committee and the Atlantic Crop Protection Committee. Each province maintains an office from which the same bulletins are available. Residents of the respective provinces should order from their own provincial office.

Nova Scotia Department of Agriculture
P.O. Box 500
Truro, Nova Scotia
B2N 5E3

Plant Industry Branch
New Brunswick Department of Agriculture
P.O. Box 6000
Fredericton, New Brunswick
E3B 5H1

Prince Edward Island Department of Agriculture
P.O. Box 2000
Charlottetown, P.E.I.
N7M 5W8

Research Station
Agriculture Canada
P.O. Box 7098
St. John's, Newfoundland
A1E 3Y3

B.C., British Columbia:
Publications Office
B.C. Ministry of Agriculture
Parliament Buildings
Victoria, British Columbia V8W 2Z7

Man., Manitoba:
Publication Section
Manitoba Department of Agriculture
411 York Ave.
Winnipeg, Manitoba R3C 3M1

Ont., Ontario
The Information Branch
Ontario Ministry of Agriculture and Food
Legislative Buildings
Toronto, Ontario M7A 1A5

Quebec:
The Information Branch
Department of Agriculture
Parliament Buildings
Quebec, P.Q. G1R 4X6

Sask., Saskatchewan:
Plant Industry Branch
Saskatchewan Agriculture
3085 Albert St.
Regina, Sask. S4S 0B1

U.S.D.A., United States Department of Agriculture:
Publications Division
Office of Government and Public Affairs
U.S. Dept. of Agriculture
Washington, D.C. 20250

Conn., Connecticut:
Agricultural Publications U-35
College of Agriculture and Natural Resources
The University of Connecticut
Storrs, Connecticut 06268
(Make any money order payable to: The University of Conn. Canadian purchases must be made payable in U.S. funds.)

Mass., Massachusetts:
Bulletin Distributions Centre
Cottage A
Thatcher Way
Amerherst, Massachusetts 01003
(Make any money order payable to: Massachusetts Cooperative Extension Service. Canadian purchases must be made payable in U.S. funds.)

Mich. Michigan:
M.S.U. Bulletin Office
P.O. Box 231
East Lansing, Mich. 48824

(Make any money order payable to: Michigan State University. Note: **Residents** of Michigan can obtain **free** single copies of up to ten different bulletins priced under 15¢. Charges are made for additional bulletins or other bulletins at prices shown. **Non-residents** of Michigan will be charged prices shown. Make money order payable to Michigan State University. Canadian purchases must be made payable in U.S. funds.)

N.Y., New York:
Mailing Room
Building Seven, Research Park
Ithaca, New York 14853
(Make any money order payable to Cornell University. Canadian residents make money order payable in U.S. funds.)

Ohio:
Section of Information and Applied
    Communications
The Ohio State University
2120 Fyffe Road
Columbus, Ohio 43210
(Note: **Residents** of Ohio may obtain one copy of any five publications free of charge. More than one copy of any bulletin or single copies of more than five bulletins may be purchased at the indicated prices. **Non-residents** of Ohio may obtain bulletins at prices indicated.
(Make any money order payable to The Ohio State University. Canadian purchases must be made payable in U.S. funds.)

Pa., Pennsylvania:
Agricultural Mailing Room
Agricultural Administration Building
University Park, P.A. 16802
(Note: **Residents** of Pennsylvania may obtain one free copy of not more than ten publications.
Non-residents should check with their own land grant university in their state. If they cannot get such publications, non-residents can request Pennsylvania publications direct from:
    Sales Supervisor
    230 Agricultural Administration
    Building
    University Park, P.A. 16802

(Make money order payable to The University of Pennsylvania. Canadian purchases must be made payable in U.S. funds.)

R.I., Rhode Island:
Publications
10 Woodward Hall
College of Resource Development
University of Rhode Island
Kingston, R.I. 02881
(Make any money order available to U.R.I. Cooperative Extension. Canadian money orders must be payable in U.S. funds.)

Glossary

Anther: The pollen-bearing top of the stamen.

Blanching: In horticulture, a process whereby light is prevented from reaching plant parts, thereby precluding the production of green chlorophyll and leaving the plant parts white. Soil, boards, tarpaper or a combination of these are used on such vegetables as leeks, celery, endive and sometimes asparagus.

Bone meal: In horticulture, an organic fertilizer made from pulverized, steamed animal bones containing approximately 2 per cent nitrogen, 11 per cent phosphorus, and no potash.

Budding: A grafting technique whereby a bud from a woody plant is placed in firm contact with the cambium layer of a compatible rootstock with a view to multiplying the budstock and obtaining desired characteristics from both the budstock and rootstock.

Cambium: A layer of live cells in the bark of a woody plant that conducts the sap.

Cane: The stem of a bush fruiting plant like a raspberry; the lateral-growing bearing branch of the grape.

Compost: A mixture of decomposed organic material. Decomposition takes place as a result of combining waste organic material with moisture, air, soil and sometimes manure or a high-nitrogen chemical fertilizer, in such a way as to produce intense bacterial activity which breaks down the organic waste into a source of humus.

Dolmitic limestone: Ground limestone rock containing approximately 80 per cent calcium carbonate and 14 per cent magnesium carbonate. Both calcium and magnesium are elements used in the growth processes of plants.

Foot candle (FC): A foot candle is a unit of illumination, equivalent to the illumination produced by a source of one candle at a distance of one foot. Light intensity drops off at the rate of the square of the distance from the source. Two feet from a fluorescent tube, the light will be one quarter of the amount at the tube itself. In SI (*Système internationale d'unités*) one foot candle equals 10.763 91 lux.

Fungicide: A chemical that kills fungus.

Germination: The sprouting of a dormant seed.

Grafting: Involves the union of the live regions of two different plants under such conditions that they will unite and grow as one.

Herbicide: A chemical that kills plants.

Humus: Soil organic material well along in the process of decomposition. In the soil it is almost constantly in a state of change by microbal activity. Soil humus is approximately 5 per cent nitrogen and 56 per cent carbon and is an important factor in the control of aeration, water-holding capacity, and granulation of soils.

Hybrid: The consistent and stable offspring of the cross-pollination of two different but compatible parent plants. The resulting variety usually exhibits a notable increase in the desirable attributes of the species involved.

Hydroponics: The growing of plants without soil. Strictly speaking, it is water culture using chemical plant nutrients but the word has come to embrace a system that uses inert materials in the chemical solution to anchor the roots.

Insecticide: A chemical that kills insects.

Loam: A soil having a relatively even mixture of the different particle sizes of sand, silt and clay plus humus and some plant nutrients (see topsoil).

Mulch: A protective ground covering (sawdust, peat moss, cocoa bean shells, crushed corn cobs, bark, straw, plastic sheet) used to reduce evaporation, prevent erosion, control weeds, protect fruit and enrich the soil.

Peat moss: Generally refers to the prepared, partially decomposed remains of sphagnum bog mosses and is used as an organic soil additive.

Perlite: A heat-expanded, lightweight form of volcanic rock that contains sodium and aluminum in amounts that can be extracted by growing plants. Perlite does not decay or deteriorate except through physical destruction. It holds water on its irregular surface areas.

Pesticide: A chemical that controls either plant diseases or insects or both.

Pistil: The female or seed-bearing organ of a flower consisting of ovary, style and stigma.

Pollination: The act or process whereby pollen is transferred from an anther to a stigma of a flower. Cross-pollination is the same process but from different flowers.

Pruning: Can be a natural process whereby a branch of a tree dies and falls off usually as the result of excessive shade. A scientific process to balance fruit production with shoot production, thereby increasing the size and quality of both. Pruning dwarfs the tree and has the localized effect of invigorating the tree.

Renovation: In horticulture, the weeding, cultivation and plant selection to a prescribed plant population, in such perennial crops as strawberries and raspberries.

Rootstock (understock): In grafting, a woody plant whose root system and lower trunk is united under controlled conditions with a scion or bud of another compatible woody plant.

Rototilling: The soil cultivating action of a motorized rotary hoe. The cultivation is achieved by the forward motion of the machine as a set of motor-driven tines or hoes rotates in the soil.

Runner: A prostrate shoot of a plant such as the strawberry which has the capability of generating new plants and/or roots at its joints.

Scion: A detached shoot of a woody plant containing two or more buds to be used in grafting. The growth characteristics of the subsequent plant will be mainly that of the scion but can be influenced by the rootstock as in dwarf fruit trees.

Solanine poisoning: Poisoning from the toxic substances which may occur in some members of the *Salanaceae* family of plants (e.g. potato).

Soluble salts: In soils, the chemical salts that will dissolve in water.

Spur: With fruit trees, a short, fruit-bearing branch.

Stamen: The male organ of the flower.

Stigma: The part of the pistil which receives the pollen.

Subsoil: That layer of soil, usually devoid of organic matter, below the soil. It may vary from fine clay to coarse gravel in content.

Suckers: Unwanted secondary shoots arising from some part of the plant or plant's root system. In fruit trees, these are called water sprouts.

Topsoil: The top layer of soil containing mineral particles of various sizes plus humus and some plant nutrients. Muck soils which occur in marshes are almost entirely organic in nature. Soil scientists have classified soil on the basis of their particle size, fine gravel being the coarsest and clay the finest (see **loam**).

Twitch grass: *Agropyrens repens* (quack, chiendent, couch grass, quitch grass, scutch grass). Perennial grass, spreading by seed and by light-coloured underground stems (rhizomes).

Vermiculite: Heat-expanded, lightweight mica ore containing some potassium and magnesium. It has a unique structure which enables it to hold and release large quantities of water and minerals for plant growth.

Whip: A young, usually unbranched, shoot of a woody plant; especially the first year's growth from a seed, graft or bud.

Index